A
Basic Grammar
of
Modern English

Bruce L. Liles
University of Missouri—St. Louis

PRENTICE-HALL, INC. Englewood Cliffs, New Jersey 07632

Library of Congress Cataloging in Publication Data

Liles, Bruce L.
  A basic grammar of modern English.

  Includes index.
  1. English language Grammar 1950- I. Title.
PE1106.L497   428'.2   78-23690
ISBN   0-13-061853-5

Printed in the United States of America

10   9   8   7   6   5   4   3   2

PRENTICE-HALL INTERNATIONAL, INC., *London*
PRENTICE-HALL OF AUSTRALIA PTY. LIMITED, *Sydney*
PRENTICE-HALL OF CANADA, LTD., *Toronto*
PRENTICE-HALL OF INDIA PRIVATE LIMITED, *New Delhi*
PRENTICE-HALL OF JAPAN, INC., *Tokyo*
PRENTICE-HALL OF SOUTHEAST ASIA PTE. LTD., *Singapore*
WHITEHALL BOOKS LIMITED, *Wellington, New Zealand*

Contents

iii

7
CLAUSES AND PHRASES THAT MODIFY NOUNS

8
PHRASES AND CLAUSES AS NOUN PHRASES

9
MOVABLE MODIFIERS

10
COMPOUNDING

Preface

This book is designed for those students whose primary interest is learning about the structures of written English rather than the methodology of a particular grammatical model. Consequently, there are no discussions of the goals of the traditionalists, structuralists, tagmemicists, stratificationalists, generative-transformationalists, Neo-Firthians, or others who have made important contributions to the study of language during this century. Each chapter describes some aspect of English, and the discussions are drawn eclectically from various grammatical models.

The book includes topics ranging from simple sentence structures to the more complex. It begins with the Subject-Verb-Object structure and proceeds to show how it may be expanded with optional adverbials, auxiliary verbs, and various kinds of modifiers. Finally, such structures as noun clauses, gerund and infinitive phrases, and compound constructions are considered. In addition to providing descriptions of these structures, the book tries to explain why we use them and why one arrangement may be better than another. Although the length of the book has been deliberately kept short, the most important structures in English are included, most of them in some detail.

It is assumed that the users of this book have a dual interest: to learn about English sentence structure and to acquire enough knowledge to enable them to apply this material. Some will be interested in studying grammar as an aid to understanding literature and as a tool for analyzing style. Others will study it for its applications to their writing or to the teaching of reading and composition. Still others who are planning to study linguistics as a discipline in itself need an understanding of the structure of English as background for more advanced work. Throughout, it is assumed that the readers have a dual interest, not just a desire to learn grammar for itself.

BRUCE L. LILES
St. Louis

1

Basic
Sentence Elements

To the average person, no single element of language is more noticeable than the word. When confronted with a mumbling speaker or poor acoustic conditions, we react with, "I couldn't understand a word." We do not say, "I couldn't understand a sentence," or comment on the unintelligibility of the phrases, clauses, or syllables.

There are various reasons for our being more conscious of words than of other elements of language. In our own speech and writing, we sometimes grope for words, or we wonder whether we are using a given term properly. We never experience a mental block for an entire sentence the way we do for a word, nor do we look sentences up in a dictionary. If we play scrabble or work a crossword puzzle, we find ourselves again searching for words, not for sentences or clauses.

We are also aware of the words that other people use. As we try to listen to a speaker talk about *epenthesis, metathesis,* and *apocope,* we realize that our unfamiliarity with the words is a hindrance to understanding the lecture. At other times we may notice that someone is using terms different from those we normally use, for example calling a carbonated beverage a bottle of *pop* when we use some other name, such as *soda, soft drink,* or *cold drink.*

Or we may question the appropriateness of a given word for some occasion. We would not be very sympathetic if we told a widow that we were sorry her husband had *croaked.* Some words do not belong to casual conversations about trivial subjects (*felicitous, salutary, enigmatic, multifarious*); others are more appropriate for conversation than for formal writing (*tacky, a dump, awful, flakey, tickled, to goof*). If a person has had too much to drink, we may refer to him or her as being *inebriated, intoxicated, drunk, plastered, polluted, soused,* and so on. These terms do not differ in meaning, but their use is restricted to appropriate contexts. Words stand out when they are either too stiff or too casual for the occasion.

Such examples as these are familiar to all of us, and they tend to make us think that language is nothing more than words. Yet there are other times when we discover that just a knowledge of words is not enough. For example, we recognize such words as *kangaroo, tourist,* and *chase* as having meanings that can be stated in a dictionary. When combined, these words take on additional meanings, depending upon how they relate to one another:

> **1.1**   The tourist chased the kangaroo.
>
> **1.2**   The kangaroo chased the tourist.

The arrangement shows whether the tourist or the kangaroo performed the act and which one was affected by it. Since we normally use words in sentences rather than by themselves, sentence structure is as important to language as words are.

For another example, every child in kindergarten knows the meanings of *I, me,* and *myself;* it is, therefore, not unfamiliarity with the meanings of these words that causes many adults to hesitate over the following choice:

> **1.3a**   There was no one there but Constance and *me.*
>
> **b**   There was no one there but Constance and *I.*
>
> **c**   There was no one there but Constance and *myself.*

In this particular instance, careful speakers and writers use the first version, *Constance and me,* since *me* is object of the preposition *but;* in others they select one of the other options:

> **1.4**   He knew that Constance and *I* were responsible.
>
> **1.5**   I bought it for Constance and *myself.*

They select *I* in **1.4** because it is a subject and *myself* in **1.5** because *I* precedes it in the same clause. It is the sentence structure that deter-

mines which pronoun (*I, me,* or *myself*) we use, not the meanings of
words.

Further dependence upon sentence structure can be illustrated
with the choice of *who* and *whom.* Some people settle for *who* at all
times, but others wish to use *whom* according to the principles followed
by careful writers. For certain sentences there is no real problem:

> **1.6** *Who* drew this delightful picture of me?
>
> **1.7** *Whom* did they nominate for president?

Others may be more confusing:

> **1.8a** *Who* did they say opened that can of worms?
>
> **b** *Whom* did they say opened that can of worms?
>
> **1.9a** *Who* do you think she saw?
>
> **b** *Whom* do you think she saw?

In **1.8,** *who* is the standard form because it is the subject of *opened;* in
1.9 it is *whom,* the object of *saw.* As with the choice of *I, me,* and *myself,* that of *who* and *whom* is governed solely by the structure of the
sentence, not by the meaning of the word.

Instead of concerning ourselves with our own usage, we may want
to consider someone else's style. Hemingway's writing is frequently
referred to as "simple" and "straightforward." These adjectives certainly seem appropriate for the following passage from his short story
"The Battler":

> He felt of his knee. The pants were torn and the skin was
> barked. His hands were scraped and there were sand and cinders
> driven up under his nails. He went over to the edge of the track
> down the little slope to the water and washed his hands. He
> washed them carefully in the cold water, getting the dirt out from
> the nails. He squatted down and bathed his knee.

Joseph Conrad, on the other hand, is often spoken of as writing in a
style that is more "complex," as illustrated by the following paragraph
from *The Secret Sharer:*

> It must be explained here that my cabin had the form of the
> capital letter L the door being within the angle and opening into
> the short part of the letter. A couch was to the left, the bed-place
> to the right; my writing-desk and the chronometers' table faced
> the door. But any one opening it, unless he stepped right inside,
> had no view of what I call the long (or vertical) part of the letter.
> It contained some lockers surmounted by a bookcase; and a few

clothes, a thick jacket or two, caps, oilskin coat, and such like, hung on hooks. There was at the bottom of that part a door opening into my bath-room, which could be entered also directly from the saloon. But that way was never used.

We easily recognize a difference between the styles of Hemingway and Conrad. We could probably identify untitled samples of their work, and we recognize imitations written by other people. We notice short, commonplace words in the Hemingway passage, but those by Conrad are not especially difficult. In addition to length, the sentences by Conrad seem more "complex" than those by Hemingway. To comment specifically on our reactions to these styles, we need to be able to talk about participial phrases, relative clauses, extraposed clauses, and the like. We shall return to these passages in Chapter 12.

Questions of usage (*who* or *whom*) and style are basically dependent upon sentence structure, not vocabulary. In this book we shall, therefore, be concerned with learning to analyze English sentences so that we can speak intelligently about them.

SUBJECTS AND PREDICATES

There are several ways in which words may relate to one another in a sentence. One of these is compounding: *bread and butter, a knife or a fork, not Rachel but Eloise.* Or we may use certain words to modify others, as when we add adjectives to *a tree* to tell what kind it is: *a tall tree, a stately tree.* Sometimes we let words cluster together in a phrase: *over the house, near the highway, beside Judy.* All of these relationships are found frequently, but one occurs more often than any of the others: the subject and predicate relationship. Because it is found in every sentence, we are starting our study with it.

There have been several definitions suggested for the subject, but none of them are very satisfactory. At times the subject is the one that performs an action, as shown by the italicized words below:

    1.10   *The repairman* knocked.

    1.11   *A woman* ran.

    1.12   *Those people* laughed.

But in other sentences the subject is the receiver of the action:

    1.13   *The curtain* tore.

    1.14   *The glass* broke.

At other times it is the person or thing that is described:

1.15 *Larry* looked bored.

1.16 *Your cousins* resemble each other.

In still other sentences it is difficult to state how the subject relates to the predicate in meaning:

1.17 *It* is snowing.

1.18 *Carol* is likely to be late.

1.19 *The medicine* was hard to swallow.

In **1.17** *it* has no real meaning. In **1.18** we are not saying that *Carol* is likely; rather, it is the entire proposition *that Carol will be late* that is likely. Similarly, we are not saying that the medicine was hard in **1.19**. Any attempt to define the subject on the basis of meaning is frustrating.

Some people have suggested that we can recognize subjects by asking "Who?" or "What?" as in these sentences:

1.20a Sandra jumped.

   b *Who* jumped?

1.21a The mattress fell.

   b *What* fell?

To follow this test, we have to know what the subject is from the start, because an alternate direction would be, "Replace the subject with *who* or *what*." Not only must we have already recognized the subject before we perform this operation; we have to know whether it names a human or not because we use *who* for humans and *what* for nonhumans. We knew, for example, to use *who* in **1.20** and *what* in **1.21**.

The most useful means of learning to recognize subjects is through examples. With only the twelve sentences we have examined so far (**1.10–1.21**), you should have no difficulty finding the subjects in the following sentences:

1.22 This shirt shrank.

1.23 His houses burned.

1.24 A man laughed.

1.25 Lucy groaned.

Wherever possible, we will avoid definitions and use examples instead.

The words following the subject are called the ***predicate,*** as shown by the italicized words below:

1.26 Harriet *coughed.*

1.27 The car *crashed.*

A predicate may consist of just a verb, as in these sentences (*coughed* and *crashed*), but there is usually more, as we shall see in the sections that follow.

In examining subjects and predicates, we should notice three features of their combination. First, we are not free to arrange them in any order that we choose. The subject normally precedes the predicate:

> **1.28a**   The flower drooped.
>
> **b**   *Drooped the flower.

The asterisk means that **1.28b** is not a possible English sentence. Although we may find similar sentences in earlier poetry, for present-day English **1.28b** is not possible. In later chapters we will see that this order is sometimes altered, such as in questions and a few other structures. However, we recognize the usual position for the subject as that before the predicate.

Second, when the verb is in the present tense, it often changes in form, depending upon whether the subject is singular or plural:

> **1.29a**   Your shoe *squeaks.*
>
> **b**   Your shoes *squeak.*

When the singular *shoe* is the subject, the verb ends in *-s: squeaks.* For the plural *shoes,* there is no ending on the verb. Agreement of subject and verb in English is usually restricted to the present tense. In the past there is no change:

> **1.30a**   Your shoe *squeaked.*
>
> **b**   Your shoes *squeaked.*

One verb is exceptional in that it shows agreement in both present and past tense. This is the verb *to be,* which has the present-tense forms *am, is,* and *are* and the past forms *was* and *were:*

> **1.31a**   I *am* here.
>
> **b**   The package *is* here.
>
> **c**   The packages *are* here.
>
> **d**   The package *was* here.
>
> **e**   The packages *were* here.

In the past tense we distinguish between *was* and *were,* according to whether the subject is singular or plural.

In addition to word order and subject-verb agreement, we recognize restrictions on which subjects may occur with certain verbs. For example, sentences **1.32–1.34** are possible, but **1.35–1.37** are not:

1.32   The referee yelled.

1.33   A diver yelled.

1.34   We yelled.

1.35   *The cup yelled.

1.36   *The geranium yelled.

1.37   *The worm yelled.

Only names of humans or a few animals may be the subject of *yell*. Some verbs permit only subjects that are concrete (*fall, jump*); others take subjects pertaining to time (*elapse*); and there are those that have still further restrictions.

DIRECT OBJECTS

Most of the sentences examined so far have contained only a verb in the predicate. There are other sentences that are not complete with just a verb:

1.38a   *The woodcarver shut.

1.39a   *Herbie insulted.

1.40a   *The hammer hit.

Something else is needed:

1.38b   The woodcarver shut *the door.*

1.39b   Herbie insulted *the passengers.*

1.40b   The hammer hit *the woman.*

The structure following the verb in each of these sentences is called a **direct object**. The predicate in each case consists of the verb and whatever follows it: *shut the door, insulted the passengers, hit the woman.*

The direct object is sometimes defined as the receiver of the action or the person or thing directly affected by it. For some sentences this definition is acceptable:

1.41   Tom chased *me.*

1.42   The teacher slapped *the student.*

1.43   Lucille threw *the eraser.*

For other sentences the object neither receives action nor is affected in any way:

1.44   Charles missed *the plane.*

1.45   The witch saw *the moon.*

1.46 Beth turned *the corner.*

1.47 The moths ate *a hole* in my coat.

Nothing happened to the plane, moon, or corner in **1.44–1.46,** nor in **1.47** do we mean that the moths were stupid enough to eat a hole instead of woolen fabric.

It has been suggested that the question words *what* and *whom* be used to locate direct objects:

1.48a Mark nodded his head.

b Mark nodded *what?*

1.49a Eloise cursed Thalia.

b Eloise cursed *whom?*

To perform this exercise correctly, one must have already located the direct object and classified it as human or nonhuman. We did not say, "Mark nodded *whom?*" or "Eloise cursed *what?*"

Through examples and a few observations, most people find that objects are as easy to recognize as subjects and verbs. To illustrate the value of the use of examples, you should try to find the direct objects in these sentences:

1.50 Henry swatted the fly.

1.51 The cook murdered his assistant.

1.52 Your son neglected his homework.

1.53 Ann waved her arm.

The objects are, of course, *the fly, his assistant, his homework,* and *her arm.*

Normally the subject precedes the verb and the direct object follows it, as in the following sentences:

1.54 The salesman shoved the customer.

1.55 The customer shoved the salesman.

We instantly recognize a difference in meaning if we interchange positions. This word order of **Subject–Verb–Object** is the most frequent in English. It is often abbreviated **SVO.**

Whenever we read or hear sentences in which this basic order is not maintained, we try to impose such an arrangement because word order is the only means we have in Modern English for indicating whether a noun is subject or object. We can illustrate our mental rearrangement of sentences by the following groups of words that do not conform to the basic pattern:

1.56 caught the man the ball

1.57 kicked the rock my cousin

1.58 the hole he dug

1.59 Perry a song sang

Most people do not just read these as lists of unpatterned words, but rather try to obtain meaningful structures. In each case the verb demands an animate subject, and only one of the nouns meets this criterion. Therefore, we are able to determine a probable subject and object for each sentence. If **1.57** had been *kicked my friend my cousin,* we would not know which of the following choices to make:

1.60 My friend kicked my cousin.

1.61 My cousin kicked my friend.

Note that in trying to arrive at a meaning for sentences **1.56–1.59,** we did not merely label one noun as subject and the other as object. We mentally rearranged them so that the subject came before the verb and the object came after it.

Even when we have other signals such as pronoun forms, we want to have the SVO order:

1.62 He understood her.

1.63 She understood him.

1.64 *He her understood.

1.65 *Understood him she.

He and *she* are subject forms, *him* and *her* object forms, as we can see from the preceding examples. Although these forms unambiguously mark the probable functions of the pronouns in **1.64–1.65,** we want the words arranged in the order of **1.62** or **1.63**.

Verbs that take direct objects are known as ***transitive verbs.*** Those that do not take objects are called ***intransitive verbs.*** Thus, the verbs in the following two sentences are transitive:

1.66 The baby *pinched* my nose.

1.67 I *cracked* the walnuts.

These are intransitive:

1.68 The vase *fell.*

1.69 The speaker *frowned.*

Once we recognize whether a verb takes an object or not, we know whether it is transitive or intransitive.

When we classify a word or group of words as a "subject" or "object," we are telling how it functions in the sentence. The same kinds of words can be used in both functions:

> **1.70**   *The fisherman* thanked *Mr. Sullivan.*
>
> **1.71**   *Mr. Sullivan* thanked *the fisherman.*

That is, any word that can function as a subject can also function as an object, and vice versa. We call words such as *fisherman, Mr. Sullivan, vase,* and *speaker* **nouns.** A noun is in turn part of a structure that we call a **noun phrase.** In the following sentences the nouns are italicized; the noun phrases to which they belong are enclosed in square brackets.

> **1.72a**   [A *butterfly*] flew away.
>
> **1.73a**   [Those miserable *fools*] hurt me deeply.
>
> **1.74a**   He saw [his former *wife*].

We may substitute a pronoun for the noun phrase:

> **1.72b**   *It* flew away.
>
> **1.73b**   *They* hurt me deeply.
>
> **1.74b**   He saw *her.*

Note that pronouns substitute for entire noun phrases, not just nouns:

> **1.72c**   *[An *it*] flew away.
>
> **1.73c**   *[Those miserable *they*] hurt me deeply.
>
> **1.74c**   *He saw [his former *her*].

Whenever a noun occurs without modifiers, we classify it as both noun and noun phrase:

> **1.75**   *Harold* helped *Betty.*

Hence, we say that *Harold* is both a noun and a noun phrase, as is *Betty.* Each noun phrase is composed of a noun or pronoun with any modifiers that accompany it.

In discussing subjects, we noticed three features: They normally precede verbs; verbs agree with them; and there are restrictions on the kinds of nouns that may function as subjects of certain verbs. There are similar features for objects. First of all, as we have seen, they normally follow the verb:

> **1.76**   The electrician shocked *the onlookers.*

Second, object pronouns are in the objective form:

> **1.77a**   She hated *him.*
>
> **b**   *She hated *he.*

Third, there are restrictions on the kinds of nouns that can function as objects of certain verbs:

>   **1.78**   Robert burned *the letters.*

>   **1.79**   *Robert burned *my industriousness.*

The object of *burn* has to be a solid, combustible substance.

PREDICATE NOUNS AND ADJECTIVES

Not all nouns that follow the verb are direct objects, as we can see from these examples:

>   **1.80**   Mr. Roberts is my tax consultant.

>   **1.81**   Mr. Roberts hit my tax consultant.

Sentence **1.81** contains the action verb *hit,* and *my tax consultant* is the direct object. In **1.80,** on the other hand, the verb does not express action, and *my tax consultant* refers to the same person as *Mr. Roberts.* We call *my tax consultant* in **1.80** a **predicate noun.** A predicate noun follows the verb and refers to the same person or thing as the subject. In **1.80,** *Mr. Roberts* and *my tax consultant* refer to the same person; in **1.81,** they are different. In only one structure does the direct object refer to the same person as the subject:

>   **1.82**   Mr. Roberts hit himself.

Whenever a direct object refers to the same person as the subject, it appears in the reflexive form with *-self* (i.e., *myself, yourself, themselves,* and the like). Except for sentences such as **1.82,** reference is a good guide for distinguishing predicate nouns from direct objects.

Adjectives can follow the verb and describe the subject, just as nouns can rename it:

>   **1.83**   He is a *fool.* (noun)

>   **1.84**   He is *foolish.* (adjective)

We call *foolish* in **1.84** a **predicate adjective.** Verbs of the senses are frequently followed by adjectives:

>   **1.85**   Your breath smells *sour.*

>   **1.86**   The bread felt *warm.*

>   **1.87**   The soup tastes *salty.*

>   **1.88**   The flowers look *lovely.*

>   **1.89**   The music sounds *heavenly.*

Some books refer to predicate nouns and predicate adjectives by the inclusive term *subjective complement.* Another term for predicate noun is *predicate nominative.* Occasionally we want to group predicate adjectives, predicate nouns, and direct objects together. When we do, we refer to them as **complements,** because they are said to "complete" the predicate.

The verb that joins a subject and a predicate noun or adjective is called a *linking* or a *copulative verb.* As with direct objects, it is the class of verb that determines whether a predicate noun or adjective is permitted or not.

Now that we have discussed three kinds of complements, let us see how we tell them apart:

> **1.90a**   The host emptied an ashtray.
>
> **1.91a**   Those students are the winners.
>
> **1.92a**   Your shoes look muddy.

Direct objects and predicate nouns being nouns, we can replace them with pronouns; we cannot make this substitution for a predicate adjective:

> **1.90b**   The host emptied *it.*
>
> **1.91b**   Those students are *they.*
>
> **1.92b**   *Your shoes look *them.*

This test works for **1.90** and **1.91,** but we see that *muddy* in **1.92** cannot be a direct object or a predicate noun because it is not a noun phrase. Further indications that *an ashtray* and *the winners* are noun phrases are the presence of the articles *an* and *the* and the fact that they can be made plural: *some ashtrays, the winners.* Since some nouns such as *honesty* and *courage* do not normally take articles or have plurals, these tests cannot be used in all cases; however, these elements are useful for recognizing nouns when they do occur.

Now that we have identified *an ashtray* and *the winners* as noun phrases, we see that they follow the verb and can, therefore, be direct objects or predicate nouns. We next see whether they refer to the same people or things as the subjects. *The host* and *an ashtray* are clearly different; hence, we call *an ashtray* a direct object. *Those students* and *the winners,* on the other hand, are the same, making *the winners* a predicate noun.

By the process of elimination we might guess that *muddy* in **1.92** is a predicate adjective, but there are better ways for determining its classification. First, it describes the subject. Second, adjectives can go before nouns as well as in the predicate-adjective position: *your muddy* *shoes.* For these reasons we know that *muddy* in **1.92** is a predicate adjective.

SUMMARY

In this chapter we have examined three basic elements of English sentence structure: subject, predicate, and complement. If the verb is intransitive, there is no complement:

> **1.93**   The audience left.

In this sentence we have only the subject *the audience* and the verb *left.* For transitive verbs, we find both a verb and a direct object in the predicate:

> **1.94**   A monkey climbed the tree.

A monkey is the subject, and *climbed the tree* is the predicate. Within the predicate we see the verb *climbed* and the direct object *the tree.* Finally, a linking verb is followed by a predicate noun or a predicate adjective:

> **1.95**   Your grandfather is a grouch.
> **1.96**   The water looked rough.

In **1.95,** *your grandfather* is the subject, and *a grouch* is a predicate noun. In **1.96,** *the water* is the subject and *rough* is a predicate adjective.

As we study other kinds of structures in later chapters, we shall find these basic functions unchanged. Here are some examples:

Subject–Intransitive Verb

> **1.97a**   Al jumped.
> **b**   Did you know [that Al jumped]?
> **c**   [Al's jumping] surprised everyone.
> **d**   It surprised everyone [for Al to jump].

Subject–Transitive Verb–Direct Object

> **1.98a**   George shook Greta.
> **b**   It delighted us [for George to shake Greta].
> **c**   Were you there [when George shook Greta]?
> **d**   George stumbled [while shaking Greta].

Subject–Linking Verb–Predicate Noun

1.99a   The carpenters are members.

   b   The carpenters [who are members] came to the meeting.

   c   [The carpenters being members], everyone was satisfied.

   d   He knows [that the carpenters are members].

Subject–Linking Verb–Predicate Adjective

1.100a   Trudy is sick.

   b   It is unfortunate [that Trudy is sick].

   c   [Trudy being sick], we cannot go.

   d   [Trudy's being sick] worries me.

The relationships expressed in the simple **a** sentences can be easily recognized in the bracketed portions of the others. The form differs from sentence to sentence, but the subjects are obvious, as are the verbs and the complements.

EXERCISES

A. In each of the following sentences either the subject-verb or the verb-object combination is inappropriate. Explain why the combination is unsatisfactory and supply a more appropriate verb.

   example: The strong winds hurt my house.

         Hurt is an inappropriate verb for *house* because it requires an animate object. *Damaged* would be a better choice.

   1. The leaves cried.
   2. I assassinated the weeds in the flower garden.
   3. She winked her ears at me.
   4. My bonds aged.
   5. Did the aspirin heal your headache?
   6. The manicurist sliced my fingernails.
   7. The leopard giggled at its prey.
   8. I embezzled a quarter from your purse.

B. Sometimes a subject-verb or a verb-object combination that would normally be inappropriate is acceptable because it makes a comparison metaphorically. For example, *roar* is a verb that originally took nonhuman subjects, such as *lion: The lion roared.* By saying

The doctor roared, we are suggesting that he made a noise like that of a lion; he could have been yelling in anger or laughing loudly. Explain the comparison that is being made in each of the following sentences:

1. The angry woman flew into the room.
2. I digested every word.
3. The cherry tree wore white for Easter.
4. The old witch cackled at me.
5. His fingers walked across the page.

C. Arrange the words from each of the following sentences in a chart like the one below:

Subject	Verb	Complement
The clown	tied	his shoe (d.o.)
They	are	worried (p.a.)

1. A bee stung me.
2. Peter fell.
3. She became afraid.
4. She became a nuisance.
5. The student felt the tremor.
6. The student felt silly.
7. The soup tasted good.
8. Hal tasted the soup.
9. Marion finished the exercise.
10. They remained friends.
11. They remained friendly.
12. The table collapsed.
13. You are a sophomore.
14. You are sophomoric.
15. You bit a sophomore.
16. The postman vanished.
17. These pearls seem expensive.
18. He bought gifts.
19. They became neighbors.
20. They visited the neighbors.

D. Write two original sentences for each of these patterns:

1. Subject–Intransitive Verb
2. Subject–Transitive Verb–Direct Object
3. Subject–Linking Verb–Predicate Noun
4. Subject–Linking Verb–Predicate Adjective

2

Adverbs and Prepositional Phrases

An English sentence is composed of a subject and a predicate, and a predicate consists of a verb and its complements. Therefore, we do not consider the following groups of words complete sentences:

> **2.1** *Left the room. (no subject)
>
> **2.2** *Agatha to Greece. (no verb)
>
> **2.3** *Bobby threw. (no direct object)

In a context that permits us to understand the intended subject, verb, or complement, we may sometimes omit these structures:

> **2.4a** "What did Carolyn do after you thanked her?" "Left the room."
>
> **2.5a** Fred went to Italy, and Agatha to Greece.
>
> **2.6a** We were playing with a baseball in the back yard. Bobby threw, and I caught.

In each of these cases the complete structure is clearly understood:

2.4b "What did Carolyn do after you thanked her?" "*She* left the room."

2.5b Fred went to Italy, and Agatha *went* to Greece.

2.6b We were playing with a baseball in the back yard. Bobby threw *it,* and I caught *it.*

These structures can be readily inserted to form complete sentences.

At times we find a simple basic sentence adequate for expressing our thoughts:

2.7 I feel tired.

2.8 We found your scarf.

2.9 Your friends left.

More often, we want to convey additional ideas. Starting with this chapter, we shall explore various ways to expand the basic sentence so that we can accommodate this other information.

ADVERBIALS OF MANNER

Instead of merely reporting that an action has occurred, we may want to tell *how* it was performed. The italicized **adverbs** in the **b** versions of the following sentences give the **manner** in which the act took place:

2.10a Betty opened the door.

b Betty opened the door *quickly.*

2.11a She answered the question.

b She answered the question *sarcastically.*

2.12a Al yelled.

b Al yelled *nervously.*

2.13a He walked.

b He walked *drunkenly.*

Each of these adverbs could be omitted, and the sentence would still be complete but less specific, as the **a** versions show.

Many adverbs of manner end in the suffix -*ly* and answer the question "How?" as we can see from the following pairs of sentences:

2.14a *How* did he ask for the money?

b He asked for it *demandingly.*

2.15a *How* did you sing?

b I sang *softly.*

2.16a *How* did they climb the stairs?

b They climbed the stairs *awkwardly*.

Each of the answers, of course, could have been limited to just the adverb, but the complete sentence is understood.

The question "How?" is not answered exclusively by manner adverbs. Predicate adjectives are also questioned with this word:

2.17a *How* are you?

b I am *happy*.

2.18a *How* did it taste?

b It tasted *delicious*.

2.19a *How* do you like this music?

b It sounds *harsh*.

There are several ways in which we can distinguish predicate adjectives from manner adverbs. First, the sentence is complete without the adverb, but the predicate adjective is essential:

2.20a We planted the garden *carefully*. (adverb)

b We planted the garden.

2.21a The garden looks *lovely*. (predicate adjective)

b *The garden looks.

Second, both adjectives and adverbs may end in *-ly*, but there is a difference in the words to which the suffix is added. When we add *-ly* to an adjective, we derive an adverb: *softly, slowly, carefully, rudely,* and the like. This suffix added to a noun, however, usually produces an adjective: *lovely, heavenly, curly, pearly, hilly,* and so on. A few words ending in the suffix *-ly* that refer to frequency may be either adjectives or adverbs: *daily, monthly, yearly, hourly.* Also, the letters *ly* at the end of some words do not constitute a suffix: *July, silly, holly, filly, tally, golly, belly.* In each case if we take off the *ly*, we do not have a word of related meaning. *Sill* and *fill* are words, but they are not related to *silly* and *filly* in the way that *quick* is related to *quickly* or *casual* to *casually*.

Although most adverbs of manner end in the suffix *-ly*, a few do not. The most common examples are *fast* and *hard:*

2.22 He ran *fast*.

2.23 He hit her *hard*.

Slow was originally like *fast* and *hard* in that it could be used as an adverb; now *slowly* has generally replaced *slow* in its adverbial sense, except in certain phrases such as "Drive slow" and "The car is idling slow."

In addition to adverbs, there are prepositional phrases that express manner. The **a** versions below contain single-word adverbs, the **b** versions prepositional phrases:

> **2.24a** They sang *gleefully*.
> **b** They sang *with glee*.
> **2.25a** We proceeded *carefully*.
> **b** We proceeded *with care*.
> **2.26a** The lion attacked the trainer *viciously*.
> **b** The lion attacked the trainer *with sudden viciousness*.
> **2.27a** He sewed on the button *awkwardly*.
> **b** He sewed on the button *with considerable awkwardness*.

A *prepositional phrase* consists of a *preposition* (*with* in these examples) and a noun, which may take modifiers (*glee, care, viciousness, awkwardness*). We can use the word *adverbial* to include both adverbs and other structures such as prepositional phrases that are used in the same way.

Adverbials of manner frequently come at the end of the sentence, but they may also be found in other positions, especially at the beginning:

> **2.28a** The student raised her hand *politely*.
> **b** *Politely*, the student raised her hand.
> **2.29a** He counted the money *without much hope*.
> **b** *Without much hope*, he counted the money.

Single-word adverbs of manner may occur between the subject and the verb:

> **2.30a** Michael refused the cake *stubbornly*.
> **b** Michael *stubbornly* refused the cake.
> **2.31a** The teacher read the names *loudly*.
> **b** The teacher *loudly* read the names.

Positioning adverbials at the beginning of the sentence or before the verb gives them more prominence than they receive at the end of the sentence. At times we place them in these positions for no other reason than to achieve variety in sentence beginnings, especially if several preceding sentences have begun with subject, then verb.

INTENSIFIERS AND SENTENCE ADVERBIALS

Similar to adverbials of manner are the **intensifiers,** also known as **adverbials of degree.** They modify adjectives and adverbs but not verbs:

> 2.32   He looked *rather* sheepish.
>
> 2.33   The horse ran *very* fast.

Some intensifiers such as *rather* and *very* do not have suffixes, but others end in *-ly* the same as manner adverbials: *extremely, completely, terribly,* and so on. In addition to not modifying verbs, they differ from adverbials of manner in that they do not come at the end of the sentence:

> 2.34   We counted the tickets *fast.* (manner)
>
> 2.35   We counted the tickets *extremely* fast. (intensifier)
>
> 2.36   *We counted the tickets *extremely.* (intensifier)

Finally, some adverbs of manner may be compared (*fast, faster, fastest; rapidly, more rapidly, most rapidly*), but intensifiers may not be.

Some intensifiers can be used in almost any situation, from the most formal to the intimately casual. *Very* is an obvious example. Others are restricted in appropriateness. *Rather* may seem stiff for certain types of conversation; *awfully,* on the other hand, is inappropriate for most kinds of writing. We may illustrate these levels as follows:

> 2.37a   I am *awfully* tired.
>
> b   I am *very* tired.
>
> c   I am *rather* tired.

Our classification of an intensifier as stilted, obscene, neutral, or casual has nothing to do with its use as an intensifier; we are merely saying that it is appropriate for certain occasions and inappropriate for others. We may refuse to use some of these words in our own speech and writing and react unfavorably to people who do use them, but they are still intensifiers.

Another class of adverbial that sometimes ends in *-ly* is the **sentence adverbial:**

> 2.38   *Naturally* she is mistaken.
>
> 2.39   *As a matter of fact,* you are too early.
>
> 2.40   *Of course* it's raining.

Unlike adverbials of manner, the basic position for sentence adverbials is at the beginning; however, they may be found elsewhere:

2.41a *Certainly* he won't be much longer.

b He *certainly* won't be much longer.

c He won't be much longer, *certainly*.

At the end of a sentence they may look like manner adverbials, but they modify the entire sentence rather than just the verb, and they are normally preceded by a comma in writing or a pause in speech. Below are two sentences, one containing an adverb of manner and the other a sentence adverb:

2.42 She sang *happily*.

2.43 She sang, *happily*.

In **2.42,** the manner adverb *happily* tells how she sang. In **2.43,** however, *happily* is a sentence adverb stating the speaker's attitude toward the action and meaning something like "It is fortunate that she sang." She may have sung sadly for all we know.

ADVERBIALS OF PLACE

Instead of telling how an action occurred, we may want to name the location with an ***adverbial of place,*** either a single word or a prepositional phrase:

2.44 Paul waited *outside*.

2.45 We saw him *upstairs*.

2.46 Cora became sick *at the party*.

2.47 She sang a song *in the living room*.

For each of these adverbials of place, we may substitute the word *there,* which is less specific in meaning. Just as there is a question word for adverbials of manner (*how*), there is also one for adverbials of place: *where*. For example, we can ask about sentence **2.44** like this:

2.48 *Where* did Paul wait?

Both adverbials of manner and place can be single adverbs or prepositional phrases, but there is a difference in frequency. Single-word adverbs of manner are found much more often than prepositional phrases are. Prepositional phrases are normally used as adverbials of manner when there is a modifier:

2.49   Bill answered *quickly*.

2.50   Bill answered *with speed*.

2.51   Bill answered *with great speed*.

That is, sentence **2.50** is less usual than **2.49** or **2.51**. For adverbials of place, however, we find the opposite order of frequency: Prepositional phrases are much more common than single adverbs. In fact, most of the single-word adverbials of place were originally prepositional phrases (e.g., *downstairs, upstairs, outdoors,* with the prepositions *down, up, out* plus a noun).

There is another difference between adverbials of manner and those of place. Whereas *with* is the most common preposition for manner phrases, there is a wider choice for place:

2.52   He stood *at* the tree.

2.53   He stood *in* the tree.

2.54   He stood *beside* the tree.

2.55   He stood *under* the tree.

2.56   He stood *behind* the tree.

2.57   He stood *in back of* the tree.

2.58   He stood *before* the tree.

2.59   He stood *in front of* the tree.

2.60   He stood *over* the tree.

Not only is there a wider choice of prepositions expressing place than manner; they also have more semantic content. The preposition *with* in the following sentence has little meaning:

2.61   He spoke *with* suspicious politeness.

The prepositions with adverbials of place, on the other hand, do have a great deal of semantic content, and we can even contrast them with one another, as examples **2.52–2.60** show.

Just as we have a complete sentence without an adverbial of manner, we can usually omit the adverbial of place:

2.62a   We baked the cake *at home*.

   b   We baked the cake.

2.63a   We rode *in a convertible*.

   b   We rode.

The meaning is less specific if we omit these adverbials, but we still have complete sentences. With some verbs, however, adverbials of place are essential:

2.64a The car was *outside.*

  b *The car was.

2.65a He lurked *outside the room.*

  b *He lurked.

2.66a Susan glanced *at the report.*

  b *Susan glanced.

2.67a I placed the vase *on the table.*

  b *I placed the vase.

We can call these **adverbial complements** because they are required.

Usually only one adverbial of place occurs with each verb; an exception can be found when the location named by one adverbial is a narrowing of the other:

2.68 We worked in the back yard under a tree.

Here both *in the back yard* and *under a tree* are adverbials of place, but *under a tree* gives a more precise location than just *in the back yard*. Whereas there are restrictions on the number of adverbials of place that may exist with a given verb, there is no problem with having both an adverbial of manner and one of place:

2.69 He drove the car hurriedly into the garage.

2.70 We went quietly into the auditorium.

Verbs that permit both manner and place adverbials will usually accept them simultaneously.

Like adverbials of manner, we normally find those of place at the end of the sentence, as we have seen in the examples. They may also occur at the beginning:

2.71a We found the box *under the bed.*

  b *Under the bed* we found the box.

2.72a We sang loudly *there.*

  b *There* we sang loudly.

Adverbials of place almost never occur between the subject and the verb:

2.72c *We *there* sang loudly.

Adverbials of manner may be found in this position, but it is rare for those of place.

ADVERBIALS OF TIME

Manner adverbials are used to tell how an action is performed, and those of place tell where. There are also *adverbials of time,* which answer the question *when.* Like other adverbials, these may be single words or phrases:

2.73 Fred earned the money *yesterday.*

2.74 He will write the letter *next week.*

2.75 I awoke *at dawn.*

Just as *there* is a general, nonspecific form for adverbials of place, *then* is the general form for time.

Like prepositions used for place, there is some semantic content in those used for time, since we can contrast them with one another:

2.76 It occurred *before* six o'clock.

2.77 It occurred *at* six o'clock.

2.78 It occurred *after* six o'clock.

2.79 He was born *in* May.

These can be contrasted with the preposition *with,* which has little semantic content when used with manner phrases.

Usually there is no more than one adverbial of time with a given verb, but, as with adverbials of place, two may exist if one is a subdivision of the other or if they are compounded:

2.80 I'll see you in the morning at six o'clock.

2.81 She worked Monday, Wednesday, and yesterday.

In **2.80,** *at six o'clock* is a narrowing of *in the morning.* If we paraphrase **2.81** as "She worked Monday, she worked Wednesday, and she worked yesterday," we have only one adverbial with each verb.

Adverbials of time co-occur freely with those of manner and place:

2.82 Bobby prepared his assignments carelessly last semester.

2.83 We traveled through the Balkans in July.

2.84 She ate sensibly at the restaurant yesterday.

Although there is some freedom with which we may arrange adverbials, the most basic word order is *manner–place–time.* Whereas some sentences permit alternate orderings, this one is possible for all. In **2.82,** we could have positioned the manner adverbial *carelessly* after the time adverbial *last summer,* but a certain amount of awkwardness would have resulted. Sentence **2.83** would have been satisfactory with the adverbials arranged so that time (*in July*) preceded place (*through the Balkans*). For **2.84,** no other order seems acceptable than the one given: manner (*sensibly*), place (*at the restaurant*), time (*yesterday*).

Like adverbials of manner and place, those of time may be shifted to the beginning of the sentence either for emphasis or for sentence variety:

2.85a They will appoint Mr. Addison *next year.*

b *Next year* they will appoint Mr. Addison.

2.86a We exchange gifts *at Christmas.*

b *At Christmas* we exchange gifts.

The adverbials we have been examining name a single time. There are others that designate frequency: *every day, in those days, frequently, often, seldom, rarely, hardly ever, sometimes,* and so on. These indicate repeated or habitual actions. Still others indicate duration: *for an hour, during the fall semester, all summer, throughout the Middle Ages,* and the like. And there are adverbials that indicate completed action, *already* being the most common.

2.87 He washed his car *yesterday.*

2.88 He washed his car *every week.*

2.89 He washed his car *all morning.*

2.90 He has *already* washed his car.

In **2.87,** we are referring to a single action at one point in time; we are not specific about when this point was within the twenty-four–hour period. In **2.88,** however, the washing did not take place at a single point in time, but on several occasions at weekly intervals. In **2.89,** we are concerned with the duration of action, and in **2.90** we see that it is completed. These different kinds of adverbials of time interact with the forms of the verb, as we shall see in the next chapter.

OTHER CLASSES OF ADVERBIALS

The most important classes of adverbials are those we have been discussing. There are several other classes ranging from a half dozen in number to twenty or thirty, depending upon the grammarian making the count. We could easily devote an entire book to adverbial classification and still not exhaust the subject or give complete analyses. For our purposes, merely illustrating some of these additional kinds will suffice:

2.91 He was angry *because of the noise.* (reason)

2.92 She wrote the message *with a pencil.* (instrument)

2.93 Louise came to the party *with Alex.* (accompaniment)

2.94 The note was written *by the headmaster.* (agent)

2.95 *If you invite us,* we will come. (condition)

Like other kinds of adverbials, some of these may occur at the beginning of the sentence as well as at the end.

In the chapters that follow, adverbials will be found frequently in the sentences that are discussed. They will need to be distinguished from adjectives and other complements; they will also be seen to interact with other elements of sentence structure.

EXERCISES

A. Arrange the words from each of the following sentences in a chart like the one below:

Subject	*Verb*	*Complement*	*Adverbial*
My uncle	mailed	the package (d.o.)	yesterday (time)

  1. Beth seemed quiet at the meeting.
  2. The children heard you this morning.
  3. Robert ordered the salad cautiously.
  4. She laughed with unwarranted nastiness.
  5. The Fishers were the victims.
  6. The maid looked puzzled then.
  7. I became a monster Monday.
  8. The road became rocky there.
  9. She snored loudly.
  10. The neighbors remained friendly.

B. Which adverbials in the preceding exercise may be moved to the beginning of the sentence? Which ones may occur between subject and verb? Are some possible but awkward?

C. Each of the following sentences contains an adverbial of manner that normally does not accompany the given verb. Explain why each one is unusual; then tell whether the combination is possible under certain conditions or always inappropriate.

  1. The dancer perspired beautifully.
  2. The doorman stumbled carefully.

    3. Beverly burped prettily.
    4. The baby docilely refused the pudding.
    5. They gulped their food daintily.
    6. Sandra cleverly forgot her money.
    7. The man encouraged me belligerently.
    8. The old man rudely died by himself.
    9. We failed the exam intelligently.
  10. Timidly he strutted out of the room.

D. Sometimes a verb by itself can convey meaning more vividly than a less specific verb with an adverb of manner can. For example, *He raced down the highway* and *He drove rapidly down the highway* may relate the same act, but *raced* is more expressive than *drove rapidly*. In the following sentences replace the general verb and manner adverbial with a more specific verb.

    1. Mike came into the room slowly.
    2. He went out of the room quietly.
    3. She told the answer in an angry voice.
    4. Robert tiredly got on the bed.
    5. He stood up silently.
    6. Gene walked to the blackboard like a duck.
    7. Ellen laughed uproariously at the joke.
    8. Rapidly he wrote the note.
    9. The cars came together with a crash.
  10. She opened the package roughly.

E. Locate the intensifiers in the following sentences and classify each as formal or informal:

    1. The children were really excited.
    2. Janice has become enormously fat.
    3. Your singing sounds bloody awful.
    4. They did it exceedingly well.
    5. Bill sneezed real loud.
    6. You were damned lucky.
    7. Your tie is devastatingly hideous.
    8. Henry threw the ball pretty hard.
    9. I am so glad that you could come.
  10. He looks totally confused.

F. Illustrate each of the following intensifiers in an original sentence and classify it as formal or informal: *simply, fabulously, just, too, undeniably, incredibly, kind of, certainly, pathetically, positively.*

G. For each of the following patterns write an original sentence containing the elements in the order that is given:

1. Subject–Verb–Direct Object–Manner
2. Subject–Verb–Predicate Noun–Time
3. Subject–Verb–Direct Object–Place–Time
4. Subject–Verb–Manner–Place
5. Subject–Verb–Intensifier–Predicate Adjective
6. Subject–Manner–Verb–Direct Object–Time
7. Time–Subject–Verb–Direct Object
8. Subject–Verb–Manner–Place–Time
9. Place–Time–Subject–Verb–Predicate Noun
10. Subject–Manner–Verb–Direct Object–Place–Time

H. Each of the following sentences contains a word ending in the letters *ly*. Classify each as an adjective, an adverb, or a noun and justify your answers.

1. He choked the cat cruelly.
2. Hank was really sorry.
3. Your cake tasted ghastly.
4. He is our ally.
5. The champagne was bubbly.
6. She felt lonely.
7. Lois dropped the hint delicately.
8. He is a bully.
9. They drink wine occasionally.
10. Your suggestion sounds beastly.

3

The Verb Phrase

A sentence contains various kinds of information, such as the meanings of the individual words and any undertones they may convey:

> **3.1**   The fireman was ostensibly looking for the hose.

We understand the main words *fireman, ostensibly, looking,* and *hose.* In addition, we realize from the use of *ostensibly* that he was probably looking for something else while pretending to hunt for the hose. With our choice of words we also indicate the level of formality we wish to convey, as seen in the following sentences:

> **3.2**   We could see a sandwich on the plate.
> **3.3**   The kids are getting sort of wild.
> **3.4**   One's selection of vocabulary affects the style of the composition.

Sentence **3.2** would be appropriate almost anywhere, but **3.3** belongs exclusively to informal conversations, and **3.4** would be more likely to appear in writing than in conversation.

In addition to the meanings of individual words and their levels of appropriateness, a sentence contains other information, such as that expressed by the relationship between subject and verb, that between the verb and its complements, or that provided by adverbials. We have seen this information illustrated in the last two chapters.

We may also want to indicate the time of an action or state, its nature (in progress, completed, recurrent), or the speaker's attitude toward it (a promise, obligation, prediction, and so on). This kind of information is expressed in part by adverbials but also by the form of the verb. We began examining adverbials in the last chapter; in this one we shall see how the verb interacts with them.

PAST TENSE

Certain adverbials of time clearly refer to past actions or states: *yesterday, last week, the year before last, in 1960*. Others may refer to the past, depending upon the time of utterance: *in January, Monday, this afternoon*. The past-tense form of the verb must accompany these adverbials. In the following pairs of sentences, the second is marked with an asterisk to indicate that it is not possible:

> **3.5a**   We moved to our new house last week.
>
> **b**   *We move to our new house last week.
>
> **3.6a**   Yesterday he opened a bank account.
>
> **b**   *Yesterday he opens a bank account.

We refer to the form of the verb as its *tense* and the meaning expressed as the *time* of the action or state.

Most verbs in English form the past tense in writing by adding the letters *-ed* to infinitives. In Chapter 8, we shall have more to say about the infinitive, but for now it will suffice to say that this is the form under which verbs are entered in a dictionary. That is, we find such entries as *eat, sleep,* and *open* — the infinitive forms — not *eats, ate, eaten, sleeps, slept, opened,* or *opens*. We can illustrate past-tense formation with a few examples:

Infinitive	*Past Tense*
look	looked
clasp	clasped
dial	dialed
pour	poured
seem	seemed
delay	delayed
sew	sewed
head	headed

With some words various spelling conventions cause additional changes: doubling a final consonant (*slap, slapped*), dropping the final *e* (*hope, hoped*), changing a final *y* to *i* (*carry, carried*), and the like. These changes result from conventions that are more general than just past-tense formation. All that is really relevant to the past tense is the ending *-ed*.

Some verbs form the past tense with *-t* rather than *-ed* and often with a change of the vowel as well:

Infinitive	*Past Tense*
buy	bought
leave	left
send	sent
bend	bent
feel	felt
mean	meant

A few verbs have two past-tense forms — one in *-ed* and one in *-t:*

Infinitive	*Past Tense*
spill	spilled, spilt
burn	burned, burnt
spoil	spoiled, spoilt

Verbs whose past tenses end in *-t* are not many, but they may occur frequently.

Verbs whose past tenses are formed with *-ed* or *-t* are known as **weak verbs.** From a historical point of view, their means of formation is an innovation that replaced an earlier process. However, they had become the largest class by the time of the earliest written records of English, and virtually all new verbs added to the language since that time have been weak.

The older type of formation is found in the so-called **strong verbs,** which show past tense by changing the vowel:

Infinitive	*Past Tense*
ride	rode
fly	flew
drink	drank
steal	stole
give	gave
stand	stood
hold	held

Even in Old English times there were fewer strong verbs than weak, and today there are no more than fifty or sixty. It is impossible to give an exact number since some (*abide, abode*) are rare and others have both strong (*thrive, throve*) and weak (*thrive, thrived*) formations. In spite of their small number, most strong verbs that survive in Modern English occur often. There is also much variation among speakers of English in the forms of strong verbs that they use.

There are still other verbs that do not easily fit into either the weak or the strong category. Such verbs as *go* (*went*) and *be* (*was, were*), whose past tenses are formed from words entirely different from the infinitives, are known as **suppletive verbs.** There are others that are peculiar in that there is no change in form between the infinitive and the past tense (*hit, cut, set, put, hurt,* and the like).

When we speak of an action in the past, we may indicate that it occurred on one or more specific occasions or that it occurred habitually:

3.7   The cat *scratched* me when I tried to pick it up.

3.8   Yesterday the cat *scratched* me twice.

3.9   The cat *scratched* me every time I tried to pick it up.

Sentences **3.7** and **3.8** illustrate specific acts, **3.9** habitual action. Often verbs denoting habitual acts can be paraphrased with *would:*

3.10   The cat *would scratch* me every time I tried to pick it up.

Such a paraphrase is not possible for specific actions. Adverbials of frequency such as *usually, normally, every day, always,* and the like may occur with verbs denoting habitual action.

PRESENT TENSE

In contrast to the past tense is the present, which is formed either with the unchanged infinitive or with the addition of -*s*. This latter form is found only with verbs whose subjects are singular nouns or the pronouns *he, she, it*. We can refer to these pronouns and nouns collectively as *third person* (i.e., the one spoken about rather than the speaker or the one spoken to). We may illustrate the third-person singular ending in a sample conjugation of the present tense:

I read	we read
you read	you read
he reads	they read

For nouns we can illustrate with *that girl* (singular) and *those girls* (plural):

that girl reads   those girls read

Since nouns that are subjects are always third person, all we have to be concerned with is whether they are singular or plural.

It is not possible to tell whether a verb is strong or weak by looking just at its present-tense forms; however, by examining the past tense, we can classify it:

Present	*Past*
grab, grabs	grabbed (weak)
wait, waits	waited (weak)
sing, sings	sang (strong)
take, takes	took (strong)
bake, bakes	baked (weak)

Because we commonly divide time into past, present, and future, it would be natural to assume that the tenses of the verb correspond to these times. We can, in fact, provide sentences in which such a correspondence exists:

3.11   I saw the snake last week. (past time, past tense)

3.12   I see the snake now. (present time, present tense)

3.13   I shall see the snake later. (future time, future tense)

The adverbs reinforce the time of the state.

However, when we change to action verbs we encounter problems with the use of the simple present tense for present time:

3.14   I break the window now.

3.15   I eat the cake now.

3.16   I catch the cat now.

These are odd, but they would be possible if we were demonstrating some process such as cooking:

3.17   Now I add two eggs.

We have, therefore, not marked them with asterisks.

If these sentences had described general truths or habitual actions, we would have found them perfectly acceptable:

3.18   I break windows now.

3.19   I eat cakes now.

3.20   I catch cats now.

In **3.18–3.20** we are not talking about specific actions, but, rather, we are commenting on our customary behavior, which contrasts in some way with our behavior in the past.

For action verbs the usual way of expressing a specific act occurring in the present is to use the present-progressive tense:

3.21   I am breaking the window now.

3.22   I am eating the cake now.

3.23   I am catching the cat now.

In a later section of this chapter we shall have more to say about progressive forms such as these. For now, we are showing that the simple present tense of action verbs normally represents habitual actions or general truths, not specific actions in present time.

When we shift to nonaction verbs, however, we do find that the simple present tense names a state that exists at the present time:

3.24   Michael looks happy now.

3.25   Now the students are friendly.

3.26   Water now covers the entire floor.

In sentences such as these we are not commenting on when the state came into being or when it will end; we are merely recognizing its existence at the present time.

Like action verbs, statives (i.e., those that name states) can refer to that which is habitual:

3.27a   Sarah knows the answer now.

   b   Sarah knows the answer every time I call on her.

3.28a   Loretta is angry.

   b   Loretta is angry all the time.

It is the adverbial that makes it clear whether present time or an habitual state is being expressed.

When we discuss events found in literature or in history, we often use what is known as the ***historical present tense.*** If we think of these events as permanently preserved in a form that keeps them fresh throughout time, we see a reason for using the present tense. Iago's deception of Othello, for example, keeps recurring every time we read Shakespeare's play; it is in a never-ending present.

FUTURE TENSE

There is, strictly speaking, no future form of the verb in English in the sense that there is in some other languages such as Latin, where we find forms like these:

vocō	I am calling
vocābam	I was calling
vocābō	I shall call

English has distinct forms for present and past (*calls, called*), but it has to add words to indicate futurity. In earlier times English grammarians tried to find equivalents for the Latin verb forms, and they said that the future tense in English is formed by adding *shall* or *will* to the infinitive: *shall call, will call.*

However, futurity in English is more often expressed by means other than by *will* and *shall*. In each of the following sentences future time is clearly meant, yet only the first of them uses *will:*

3.29   The sale will end tomorrow.

3.30   The sale ends tomorrow.

3.31   The sale is going to end tomorrow.

3.32   The sale should end tomorrow.

3.33   The sale could end tomorrow.

3.34   The sale must end tomorrow.

We could easily find even other means of expressing future time. The adverb *tomorrow* can function with several helping verbs to mark futurity; in fact, it can even be used with the present-tense form, as **3.30** shows. The present form is also used in dependent clauses that accompany main clauses containing future tense:

3.35   We will see him when he *gets* here.

3.36   When you *leave,* please turn out the lights.

The future forms *will get* and *will leave* are not possible in dependent clauses such as these.

When we speak of past events, we usually state them as facts, whether we witnessed them personally or learned about them from our reading or from other speakers. We can also refer to events in the present as factual. For the future, on the other hand, our statements always take the form of promises, predictions, and the like. Although we may feel confident that our expectations about the future will come about, we never can speak of them with the same certainty that we do of the past. An obvious example can be seen in this sentence:

> **3.37** It will rain this afternoon.

We are unquestionably talking about a future event, but we are making a prediction about it, not giving a neutral fact.

MODALS

Let us examine more closely the ways in which we talk about the future. First of all, we may make a prediction:

> **3.38** Charles will be in the cafeteria on time.
> **3.39** We shall find him unharmed.

Will and *shall* can also be used to make promises about the future:

> **3.40** I shall return.
> **3.41** We will do your work for you.

Other helping verbs express obligation:

> **3.42** You must tell her the combination.
> **3.43** She should brush her hair more often.
> **3.44** Someone ought to change these rules.

Still others indicate a possibility:

> **3.45** You may find the car already sold.
> **3.46** It might snow tonight.

There are nine helping verbs in English that are usually called **modals:** *may, might, can, could, will, would, shall, should,* and *must.* There are also a few marginal modals, such as *ought.* Each of these can be used to refer to the future while expressing ideas such as possibility, obligation, and the like. As we shall see in an exercise at the end of this chapter, each one has more than one meaning.

In addition to future time, modals may be used to express past time, present time, and habitual actions:

> **3.47** I could wear a size eight shoe then. (past)
> **3.48** We can hear you well. (present)
> **3.49** He would smirk every time he saw us. (habitual)
> **3.50** You might be surprised tomorrow. (future)

They are not limited to use with future time.

The verb that follows a modal is always in the infinitive form. We can see that it does not contain tense by examining a few examples:

3.51a He should eat the carrots.

 b *He should eats the carrots.

 c *He should ate the carrots.

We do not change the verb following a modal for tense. Where, then, is tense expressed in sentences with modals? As we have seen, some modals refer to any time:

3.52 He could hear the announcement. (past)

3.53 He could do it now. (present)

3.54 He could drive her to the airport tomorrow. (future)

It would be tempting to say that there is no tense in a sentence containing a modal. Yet grammarians have traditionally said that every sentence must contain tense, and they have usually determined the tense of modals on etymological grounds:

Present	*Past*
may	might
can	could
will	would
shall	should
	must

The present tense of *must* was *mote*, which became obsolete after the sixteenth century. The final *t* or *d* on *might, could, would, should,* and *must* was originally a past-tense marker. Regardless of the time of the action or state, the tense of a modal is determined by its form.

Sometimes modals express conditions contrary to fact, as in the following sentence:

3.55 If I could communicate with the dead, I would be happy.

The speaker cannot communicate with the dead, as indicated by the use of *could.* Conditions contrary to fact may also be expressed by the **subjunctive mood** of the verb, which in English is identical to the past tense:

3.56 If I *had* wings, I could fly to the moon.

3.57 What would you do if you *met* a mugger tonight?

3.58 If he *borrowed* my car, I would be angry.

3.59 If Judith *were* more astute, she would ignore you.

For *be,* the subjunctive is *were* regardless of whether the subject is singular or plural, as we see in **3.59.**

Not all clauses beginning with *if* indicate conditions contrary to fact. Some, like **3.60,** describe a condition that may be true:

3.60   If you are telling the truth, I will apologize.

3.61   If you were telling the truth, I would apologize.

In **3.60,** I am saying that you may be telling the truth, but in **3.61** I have accepted your statement as a lie.

PROGRESSIVE ACTION

Unless they name habitual actions or general truths, verbs of action normally refer to completed acts:

3.62   Sally cursed me.

3.63   The postman rang the doorbell.

3.64   We wrote the letter.

At times we want to comment on an action in progress:

3.65   Susan *was washing* her hair when the telephone rang.

3.66   I *was singing* in the shower when he entered the room.

3.67   Ron *is changing* a flat tire.

3.68   Terry *will be practicing* a Chopin etude when you see him.

In each sentence we are speaking of an action in progress without regard to its beginning or end, and we are also relating it to another act. In **3.65,** the act of shampooing was in progress when another past action took place: the ringing of the telephone. Similarly, in **3.66** the singing and the entering were contemporaneous, the singing being in progress. In **3.67,** the act of changing the tire is in progress with regard to the time of speaking. In **3.68,** the progressive verb relates to another future action: your seeing Terry.

To form ***progressive verbs,*** we use the auxiliary (helping) verb *be,* the exact form depending upon the subject and the tense:

3.69a   I *am* watching you.

b   I *was* watching you.

3.70a   You *are* getting on my nerves.

b   You *were* getting on my nerves.

3.71a   She *is* standing by the duck pond.

b   She *was* standing by the duck pond.

The verb following the auxiliary *be* has the ending *-ing;* we call such verbs *present participles.* We can state the rule for forming progressive verbs, then, as follows: Use the auxiliary *be* and make the main verb a present participle. As we can see from the above examples, tense is expressed by *be: am* vs. *was; are* vs. *were; is* vs. *was.* The main verb remains unchanged: *watching, getting, standing.*

So far we have seen sentences with just the main verb and no auxiliaries, those with modals, and those with *be:*

3.72   The dogs barked loudly.

3.73   The dogs could bark loudly.

3.74   The dogs are barking loudly.

It is possible to have both a modal and the auxiliary *be* with the same verb:

3.75   You should be studying chemistry.

3.76   They will be staying up all night.

3.77   Hank may be riding with Emma to the party.

We are adding to the notion of progressive action that of obligation (**3.75**), prediction (**3.76**), or possibility (**3.77**). When a verb has both a modal and a form of *be* with it, the modal always comes first, and it indicates the tense. When a modal precedes, *be* is in the infinitive form, the same as any other verb that follows a modal.

THE PERFECT TENSES

The progressive tenses are used to indicate the occurrence of an action at the same time as another action or state. We can also show that an action was completed at the time another act took place. We use the *perfect tenses* for this purpose:

3.78   Greg *had written* the letter when I saw him.

3.79   Greg *has written* the letter.

3.80   Greg *will have written* the letter when you see him.

In **3.78,** the act of writing was completed before the act of seeing occurred. In **3.79,** it was completed before the time the sentence was spoken (i.e., the present). The time of completion in **3.80** is in the future, prior to the act of seeing. It should be pointed out that the perfect tenses do not indicate just completed action, because that is normally expressed by the simple tenses of action verbs:

3.81   Greg wrote the letter.

In **3.81,** the act of writing was completed, the same as in **3.78–3.80.**

The difference is whether a point in time other than the present is established or not.

For the simple tenses, the only focal point is the present, from which we judge other actions as past or forthcoming. For the past perfect tense we set up an additional focal point in the past and say that another act was completed before that time. This is similar to the past progressive, in which we say that an act was in progress at the time of another past action. Similarly, for the future perfect we are commenting on an action that will be completed before another focal point in the future. Let us illustrate these points in time:

    3.82   The chair had collapsed before I touched it.

The time of utterance is the first time with which we are concerned, that is, the present. We say that the act of touching occurred before the time of utterance; hence, it is given in past tense (*touched*). It is also set up as a second focal point. The third point is that of collapsing, which is previous to that of point two, the touching. We can represent these three times linearly:

3	2	1
collapsing	touching	speaking

Unlike the simple tenses, which have only two points of reference — the time of speaking and the time of the verb in question — the past and future perfect tenses have three.

For the present perfect tense there are only two points in time — that of the utterance and that of the completed action:

    3.83   The birds have flown away.

Since we have these same points for the simple tenses, there is little difference in meaning between the present perfect and the simple past:

    3.84a   Chuck has read your essay.
       b   Chuck read your essay.
    3.85a   We have found her address.
       b   We found her address.

In both versions of each sentence the act was completed at some time before the time of the utterance. There is a difference, however, when we use a perfective adverb such as *already:*

3.86a I have already seen that movie.

b ?I already saw that movie.

Whereas everyone accepts an adverb such as *already* with a perfect tense, many find it questionable or even impossible with a simple tense.

The perfect tenses are formed with the auxiliary *have.* The verb following *have* is a *past participle,* which for weak verbs ends in -*ed* or, for a few verbs, -*t* and is identical in form to the past tense:

3.87a Harold *has opened* the window.

b Harold *had opened* the window.

3.88a We *have tasted* the cheese.

b We *had tasted* the cheese.

It is the auxiliary that changes for tense; the main verb remains a past participle. For future time we use *will have* or *shall have* plus the past participle:

3.89 They *will have left* before we get there.

3.90 I *shall have finished* it by then.

Strong verbs occasionally have the same form for the past participle as that for the past tense:

3.91a He *stood* there for an hour.

b He had *stood* there for an hour.

3.92a We *dug* in the garden.

b We have *dug* in the garden.

For most strong verbs, however, there is a difference between the past tense and the past participle. Here are a few examples:

Infinitive	Past Tense	Past Participle
drive	drove	driven
choose	chose	chosen
begin	began	begun
break	broke	broken
eat	ate	eaten
take	took	taken
know	knew	known

Many strong verbs have past participles ending in -*en,* but with the vowel we find as much diversity in the formation of past participles as we did in that of past tenses.

When the auxiliary *have* co-occurs with a modal before a verb, the modal comes first:

    3.93a   You could have helped me.

      b   *You have could helped me.

As we noticed earlier in this chapter, the verb following a modal is always in the infinitive form; hence, we find *have*, not *had* or *has*, in **3.93a**. Also, the verb following the auxiliary *have* is a past participle: *helped*. The combination of modal plus *have* does not provide a meaning of completed action plus the meaning of the modal; rather, this is the way in which we often express past time with modals;

    3.94a   You could prevent the accident. (present time)

      b   You could have prevented the accident. (past time)

    3.95a   They must be tired. (present time)

      b   They must have been tired. (past time)

Time is not expressed by changes in the forms of verbs in structures such as these.

    The auxiliary *have* may also co-occur with the auxiliary *be:*

    3.96a   We have been working.

      b   We had been working.

    3.97a   She has been humming.

      b   She had been humming.

As these examples illustrate, it is the first auxiliary, *have*, that shows tense. When both *have* and *be* are used as auxiliaries with the same verb, *have* precedes *be*. The observations we made earlier about the forms of the verbs following these auxiliaries hold true when they are used together. That is, *have* is followed by a past participle (*been*), and *be* is followed by a present participle (*working, humming*).

    It is also possible to have all three auxiliaries—modal, *have*, and *be*—with one verb:

    3.98   Trudy should have been working harder.

    3.99   You must have been eating garlic.

    3.100   They might have been eavesdropping.

The order is modal, then *have*, then *be*. Tense is expressed by the first auxiliary. The auxiliary *be* is followed by a present participle (*working, eating, eavesdropping*); *have* is followed by a past participle (*been*); and the modal is followed by an infinitive (*have*).

When all possible auxiliaries are found in a sentence, they come in the order modal, then *have,* then *be;* we may omit one or more, but we must retain this order:

		Modal	*have*	*be*	
3.101	We	might	have	been	going
3.102	We	should	have		gone
3.103	We	must		be	going
3.104	We	shall			go
3.105	We		have	been	going
3.106	We		had		gone
3.107	We			are	going
3.108	We				went

The verb following the modal is always an infinitive: *have* in **3.101** and **3.102,** *be* in **3.103,** *go* in **3.104.** Following *have* is a past participle: *been* in **3.101** and **3.105,** *gone* in **3.102** and **3.106.** The verb following *be* is a present participle: *going* in **3.101, 3.103, 3.105,** and **3.107.** The first word in the verb phrase carries the tense: the modal in **3.101–3.104,** *have* in **3.105** and **3.106,** *be* in **3.107,** and the main verb in **3.108.** The forms of the verb phrase, as we can see, can be stated very simply. The changes in meaning that result from alterations in form are much more complex.

VARIATION IN VERB FORMS

Because there is variation in the forms of some verbs, it seems appropriate to comment on these differences. This variation is limited almost exclusively to the fifty or so strong verbs in Modern English. For the thousands of weak verbs, all speakers of English use the same forms. In some environments, especially before a word beginning with *t,* there may be a question about whether we pronounce the *-ed* ending on the past tense or past participle:

3.109   He *raced* to the finish line.

However, we think we are pronouncing it, and listeners "hear" it, whether it is actually present in the acoustic signal or not. Apart from questioning whether the *-ed* is really pronounced in some environments, there is no problem with weak verbs. No one uses a past tense or past participle of *close* other than *closed.* It would be unthinkable for anyone to use forms such as *cloose, clase, clise,* or the like. Since well over ninety percent of the verbs in anyone's vocabulary are weak, it is only a small percentage of verbs—the strong category—that show variation. Yet many strong verbs are used with such high frequency that they stand out more prominently than their percentage would suggest.

Since Old English times many originally strong verbs have become weak. If *glide* had remained strong, the principal parts would now be *glide, glode, glidden* or *glide, glid, glidden.* For all speakers of English, this verb has become weak. Some other verbs that have changed categories are *creep, chew, burn, climb,* and *help.* Some have retained both strong and weak formations. *Wake* and *awake,* for example, have strong forms (*woke, awoke*) and weak (*waked, awaked*). Some of these that have both formations have developed different meanings for the two. For many people the weak formation of *hang* (*hanged*) is used for executions, whereas the strong formation *hung* is used for other purposes. These people would say:

3.110 We *hanged* him, and then he *hung* there.

Another verb of this nature is *shine.* With the weak formation it is transitive, but when strong it is intransitive:

3.111 We *shined* our shoes until they *shone.*

Abide may have both kinds of formation, but most people use this verb so rarely that neither *abode* nor *abided* seems especially natural. *Thrive* is another example like this.

As a change in a language spreads, it may eventually reach all speakers, such as the conversion of *creep* and *glide* to the weak category. Some changes do not spread uniformly, either because certain groups of people are not exposed to them or because they intentionally reject them. In some places the strong past tenses *clumb* and *holp* survived much longer than in others, but the changes to the weak *climbed* and *helped* seem to be winning out now. For these verbs standard English is less conservative than certain other dialects. The opposite condition also exists for such verbs as *know* and *grow,* which standard English has retained as strong but which have become weak in some other dialects: *knowed* and *growed.* Neither standard English nor the other dialects are equally conservative with all verbs, although the tendency in all varieties of the language is to move from the strong category to the weak, not the other way around.

Another change that has been spreading is the loss of the past participial ending *-en* on strong verbs. For all speakers of English it has been lost on *grind, wind, slide,* and several others. For a few verbs the

-*en* form survives when the past participle is a modifier but not when it is a verb:

3.112a He has *drunk* his milk.

  b He is a *drunken* fool.

3.113a His shirt has *shrunk*.

  b He collects *shrunken* heads.

3.114a The treasure has *sunk*.

  b He is looking for *sunken* treasure.

And we speak of *cloven* hooves but do not say that we have *cloven* something in two parts.

For some people additional verbs have lost their past participial ending -*en* so that they say *have rode, have rose, have spoke, have froze, have broke,* and the like. By the seventeenth century many verbs had lost their -*en* endings; the examples in the preceding sentence can all be found in Shakespeare or Milton. Standard English has restored the ending on some of the past participles, but certain other dialects have not. No dialect of English, including the standard, is consistent in retaining or dropping -*en* on all past participles of strong verbs.

The past participle of *get* is interesting in that is has the two forms *have got* and *have gotten* in American English, whereas British English has only *have got*. For Americans the two are not usually interchangeable. With the meaning *must,* one may say either *I have to go* or *I have got to go,* but not **I have gotten to go. Gotten* never occurs when *have* can stand alone, as in the preceding example. For the meaning *receive,* Americans normally use *gotten* (*They have gotten some new shoes*).

One of the most noticeable changes in English is the merger of principal parts of strong verbs. In Old English each strong verb had four principal parts, but by Early Modern English times these had been reduced to three at most, as illustrated by the following:

Infinitive	*Past Tense*	*Past Participle*
sing	sang	sung
ring	rang	rung
see	saw	seen
speak	spoke	spoken
fly	flew	flown

For some verbs the past tense and the past participle have merged, leaving only two distinct forms:

Infinitive	Past Tense/ Past Participle
spin	spun
cling	clung
slide	slid
wind	wound

Some verbs with the vowel *i* followed by *ng* or *nk* are currently under-going a merger of principal parts. The older past tense of *cling* (*clang*) is no longer heard, but the following exhibit much variation and con-fusion even among well-educated speakers of English: *slink, stink, shrink, swing, fling, wring,* and a few others. *Drink* for many people has the past tense *drank* and the past participle *drunk.* Others use *drank* for both forms. For some dialects other than standard English, there are still other verbs that have merged the past tense and the past participle: *he ate, he has ate; she seen it, she has seen it; she saw it, she has saw it; he wrote, he has wrote; she taken, she has taken;* and the like. To the linguist such variants are interesting examples of change in the language that has been extended to more verbs in some dialects than in others. To other people, the strong verb forms that people use reveal their regional or social origins; and depending upon their atti-tudes toward these origins, the forms will be looked upon with favor, interest, amusement, or disdain.

EXERCISES

A. Draw a chart like the one given below and enter each word from the verb phrase in the appropriate column. Do nothing with the other elements of the sentence.

example: We had been running for over an hour.

Modal	Have	Be	Verb
—	had	been	running

1. Harriet was writing a novel.
2. That faucet has been leaking for two days.
3. You must have been the last one.
4. They should have been sleeping.
5. The hawk flew out of sight.
6. The troops have arrived.
7. The dog might have been hiding from us.
8. He can have the money.
9. They could have traded the car.
10. We shall be waiting here.

B. Arrange the words from each of the following sentences in a chart like the one below:

Subject	Verb	Complement	Adverbial
Wanda	was reading	a book (d.o.)	at school (place)

1. The neighbors have bought a motorcycle.
2. Those remarks seem perfectly ridiculous.
3. The building would have collapsed some time.
4. That dog has grown more friendly recently.
5. We are selling our car impulsively.
6. Freddie wrote a check.
7. Those men must have been cousins.
8. My tailor has become a new person.
9. My tailor has made a new suit.
10. Mark will build it outside.

C. Explain why these sentences are not possible:

1. *We washed the windows tomorrow.
2. *After we had found the mistake, we correct it.
3. *Last December she practices every day.
4. *Barbara claps her hands when she saw the doll.
5. *He will thank you after you had helped him.
6. *She was typing a letter when Annette has entered the room.
7. *Since you have been so nasty, I had not given you a birthday present.
8. *If you should go, I am sad.
9. *The Smiths will be packing their suitcases when you have seen them.
10. *Napoleon has died in 1821.

D. Rewrite the following sentences using each of the five forms given below.

example: The cat spilled the milk.

a. Present progressive: The cat is spilling the milk.
b. Past progressive: The cat was spilling the milk.
c. Present perfect: The cat has spilled the milk.
d. Past perfect: The cat had spilled the milk.
e. Future with *may:* The cat may spill the milk.

In some sentences one or more of these forms will not be possible. Explain why. Then explain how the other versions differ in meaning.

     1. I raked the leaves yesterday.
     2. Henry jogged all Saturday afternoon.
     3. We return home next week.
     4. The roast tastes delicious to your friends.
     5. Your children are noisy.

E. Write a sentence for each of the following patterns:

1. Subject–Past–Verb–Direct Object–Manner
2. Subject–Present–*be*–Verb–Intensifier–Predicate Adjective
3. Subject–Past–*be*–Verb–Direct Object–Place
4. Subject–Present–*have*–Verb–Place–Time
5. Time–Subject–Past–*have*–Verb–Predicate Noun
6. Place–Subject–Present–*have*–*be*–Verb–Manner
7. Subject–Past–*have*–*be*–Verb–Direct Object
8. Subject–Present–Modal–Verb–Predicate Noun–Time
9. Subject–Past–Modal–*be*–Verb–Predicate Adjective
10. Sentence Adverb–Subject–Present–Modal–*have*–*be*–Verb–Place

F. Explain how the following pairs of sentences differ in form and in meaning:

  1a. The children are chasing a frog.
    b. The children were chasing a frog.
  2a. You should be more careful next time.
    b. You will be more careful next time.
  3a. Randy wrote the last page of his paper.
    b. Randy had written the last page of his paper.
  4a. We were dusting the furniture.
    b. We had dusted the furniture.
  5a. The men will consider the suggestion this afternoon.
    b. The men will be considering the suggestion this afternoon.
  6a. That must be the wrong telephone number.
    b. That must have been the wrong telephone number.
  7a. Weldon might have been thinking about Cathy.
    b. Weldon might be thinking about Cathy.
  8a. Marilyn has been calling you.
    b. Marilyn had been calling you.
  9a. You would be disappointed with that choice.
    b. You would have been disappointed with that choice.
 10a. I would be glad to recommend you for the position.
    b. I will be glad to recommend you for the position.

G. For each of the following sentences, give the time that is understood for the action (i.e., not the tense). How do you know?

1. Bears hibernate during the winter.
2. Rick knows the answer.
3. Darlene is tall.
4. That will be enough of that nonsense!
5. Are you going to spend the night?
6. Will you spend the night?
7. That will be $16.50, please.
8. She has three grandchildren.
9. Mike is working in San Francisco.
10. By leaving early, you would make a fool of yourself.

H. Fill in the blank with each of the modals: *may, might, can, could, will, would, shall, should, must.* How do the nine versions differ in meaning?

Joan _____ play the piano.

I. Each of the following sentences has more than one meaning, depending upon how we interpret the modal. Give each of these meanings.

1. You might know that he is not able to add.
2. You will answer the questions correctly.
3. That must be our classroom.
4. He may go to bed early tonight.
5. John could play the violin.
6. You can go to the devil.
7. She would wear her oldest dress to the party.
8. We should be happy to go with you.

J. Why do many people prefer the second sentence to the first one?

1. An example of an article would be *the.*
2. An example of an article is *the.*

K. Fill in the blank of each sentence with the standard past tense or past participle of the verb in parentheses. If you are in doubt about which form is used in standard English, consult a good dictionary; do not just guess.

1. She _____ the horn at me. (blow)
2. They have already _____ all the coffee. (drink)
3. We _____ down to rest for a few minutes. (lie)
4. They _____ their coats on the bed. (lay)
5. He _____ about where he had been. (lie)
6. The children _____ in the yard. (swing)
7. The criminal has probably _____ away by now. (get)
8. You should have _____ under the dryer. (sit)

9. They must have _____ the baby down on the bed. (set)
10. He _____ another piece of cake. (take)
11. They have _____ away. (fly)
12. This shirt _____ when I washed it. (shrink)
13. The shoe _____ me perfectly. (fit)
14. We had _____ before we heard the news. (rise)
15. We had _____ our arms before we heard the news. (raise)
16. Sarah has _____ her job again. (quit)
17. Something _____ in the store. (stink)
18. They have _____ often in the lake. (swim)
19. They had already _____ the prisoner. (hang)
20. The water pipes have _____. (burst)
21. He _____ into the river. (dive)
22. The noise _____ me very early this morning. (wake)
23. We _____ to do better. (strive)
24. She _____ her shoes under the bed. (fling)
25. We have _____ our point. (prove)

4

Variations in Basic Word Order

Among the devices used to indicate syntactic structures in English, none is more important than word order. Auxiliary verbs always precede the main verb, and they themselves are ordered so that modals precede *have,* and *have* precedes *be.* There is also a basic ordering for subjects, objects, and verbs; violation of this order may affect the meaning of the sentence or else produce a group of words whose syntactic relationships are unclear:

> **4.1**   Frank saw Carolyn at the bank.
> **4.2**   Carolyn saw Frank at the bank.
> **4.3**   *Frank saw at the bank Carolyn.
> **4.4**   *Frank Carolyn at the bank saw.

There are times when we wish to vary the word order of a sentence to avoid monotony, or we may want to give special emphasis to a particular word or phrase. To do so, we have several ways of changing the basic order and retaining the original meaning. These variations will be the subject of this chapter.

ADVERBIALS

As we saw in Chapter 2, the basic position for adverbials of time is after the complement:

> **4.5** Harriet opened a bank account *last week*.
>
> **4.6** He will be our treasurer *for the next two months*.

They occur immediately after intransitive verbs:

> **4.7** This battery should last *one year*.

For emphasis, contrast, or variety, adverbials may be moved to the beginning:

> **4.8a** Mike showed me the picture *this morning*.
>
> **b** *This morning*, Mike showed me the picture.
>
> **4.9a** You will be sorry *some day*.
>
> **b** *Some day* you will be sorry.
>
> **4.10a** The museum will close *in an hour*.
>
> **b** *In an hour*, the museum will close.

With intransitive verbs, movement of the adverbial to the beginning is sometimes permissible, as in **4.10.** In other sentences, especially with adverbials of duration, the results are less acceptable:

> **4.11a** You should go on a diet *for six weeks*.
>
> **b** *For six weeks* you should go on a diet.

Although some speakers of English accept **4.11b,** others find it questionable.

Movement of the adverbial from its basic position at the end to the beginning of a sentence is possible for adverbials other than those of time. For example, we do the same thing with adverbials of place:

> **4.12a** They solved the problems *at home*.
>
> **b** *At home* they solved the problems.
>
> **4.13a** We felt out of place *there*.
>
> **b** *There* we felt out of place.

Adverbials of manner and instrument are also movable:

> **4.14a** Frank unscrewed the lid *carefully*.
>
> **b** *Carefully*, Frank unscrewed the lid.
>
> **4.15a** You can open any door in the hotel *with this key*.
>
> **b** *With this key* you can open any door in the hotel.

And we can move adverbials of reason:

4.16a   We felt uncomfortable *because of the humidity.*

   b   *Because of the humidity* we felt uncomfortable.

4.17a   I fell to the ground *because someone pushed me.*

   b   *Because someone pushed me,* I fell to the ground.

Adverbials of time are not the only ones that are movable.

Let us look more closely at what we accomplish by moving an adverbial to the front of the sentence. We often make this change for emphasis and contrast:

4.18a   I thought the prices were high in New York, but they were outrageous *in Paris.*

   b   I thought the prices were high in New York, but *in Paris* they were outrageous.

4.19a   I can't see you today, but I will listen to your problem *tomorrow.*

   b   I can't see you today, but *tomorrow* I will listen to your problem.

Sometimes there is no contrast, but we want to stress the adverbial:

4.20a   Your rent will be due *on the first of next month.*

   b   *On the first of next month* your rent will be due.

4.21a   You are to turn left *at the next intersection.*

   b   *At the next intersection* you are to turn left.

Both sentences in each group have the same basic meaning, but **4.20b** and **4.21b** give more importance to the adverbial than the **a** versions do. There are still other occasions on which we do not emphasize the adverbial but place it first to break up the monotony of a series of sentences all beginning with subject plus verb.

It is customary to place a comma after a long introductory adverbial modifier, but we do not usually set off such modifiers when they come at the end of the sentence:

4.22a   *When the water started leaking from the upstairs bedroom into the living room,* I decided to call the plumber.

   b   I decided to call the plumber *when the water started leaking from the upstairs bedroom into the living room.*

There is usually no comma after a short introductory adverbial:

4.23a   *In June* the Millers moved to Utah.

   b   The Millers moved to Utah *in June.*

The decision as to what is "long" and what "short" is often not so clear as in the examples just given. At one time some grammarians rather arbitrarily called a modifier of five words or more long and one under five words short. However, it takes only a few minutes' inspection of books and magazines from major publishers to show that there is much variety in actual practice for modifiers of medium length. The only honest statement that can be made about current practices is that a comma is placed after a long introductory adverbial modifier but not after a short one. For those of medium length the comma is optional.

At times there are other reasons for placing a comma after an introductory modifier. The most obvious of these is to clarify the syntactic structure:

>   **4.24**   Below the ground was frozen.

Below could be an adverb or a preposition, but here it is clearly an adverb. If we begin reading the sentence thinking that *below the ground* is a prepositional phrase, we are jarred with the verb *was,* which seemingly has no subject. We then retrace our analysis of the sentence to derive an acceptable structure and meaning:

>   **4.25**   Below, the ground was frozen.

Here we are using a comma after an adverbial modifier not because of its length but because we wish to prevent misreading.

The statements we have been making apply only to adverbials of time, place, manner, and the like. Sentence adverbials, including transitional words and phrases, are normally followed by commas regardless of their length:

>   **4.26**   *Of course,* you will have trouble starting your car.
>   **4.27**   *Certainly,* it will be good to see her again.
>   **4.28**   *However,* they are seldom on time.

These sentence modifiers are also set off by commas if they are moved to other positions in the sentence.

QUESTIONS

We often ask questions that differ from statements only in their intonation pattern, which is represented by a question mark in writing:

>   **4.29**   You are going with us?
>   **4.30**   No one tried to stop her?

This is the form for the so-called "echo question," which means something like "Did you say ...?" or "Do you mean ...?"

    4.31   Carl proposed to *Evelyn?*

    4.32   This is good?

Questions of this type may be mere requests for information, or they may reflect sarcasm or incredulity. Whatever their meaning, their word order is the same as that of statements.

    Usually there is an alteration in word order to indicate that the sentence is a question. Instead of the order of **4.29,** we may find:

    4.33   Are you going with us?

Here we have not only the intonation pattern of the question, but also the inversion of *are* and *you*. In statements we find the subject first, then the verb with its auxiliaries. In questions we find something in front of the subject.

    The last sentence is vague because we used the word *something* instead of a more specific word, such as *verb*. If we look at **4.33,** we see that the main verb *going* is still positioned after the subject. Only the auxiliary *are* precedes. If we look at an additional sentence, we see that it is not the entire auxiliary that precedes, but only part of it:

    4.34   Could they have been cheating?

Here there are three auxiliary verbs, but only one of them goes before the subject. As speakers of English we have no trouble forming questions, and we readily recognize one that is poorly formed:

    4.35   *Could have they been cheating?

This is not a possible English sentence, hence the asterisk. There is a considerable gulf between our knowledge of how to form questions and our ability to make this knowledge explicit enough to explain what we are doing.

    To determine exactly what it is we place before the subject when we form questions, let us examine several sentences.

    4.36a   The farmer *has* plowed the north field.

      b   *Has* the farmer plowed the north field?

    4.37a   He *can* unlock the door.

      b   *Can* he unlock the door?

    4.38a   You *were* dancing at the wedding.

      b   *Were* you dancing at the wedding?

In these sentences it is the entire auxiliary that precedes the subject, whether it is a modal or a form of *have* or *be*. Now let us look at some sentences with two auxiliaries:

4.39a   The cat *has* been chasing a mouse.

b   *Has* the cat been chasing a mouse?

4.40a   They *would* have sold the car.

b   *Would* they have sold the car?

4.41a   She *will* be earning a good salary.

b   *Will* she be earning a good salary?

Now it is only the first auxiliary that precedes the subject, either *have* or a modal. Finally, we should examine some sentences with three auxiliaries:

4.42a   I *should* have been more careful.

b   *Should* I have been more careful?

4.43a   They *could* have been practicing.

b   *Could* they have been practicing?

Again it is the first auxiliary that is fronted. We are now ready to state what it is that goes before the subject in a question: the first auxiliary. When there is only one auxiliary, as in **4.36–4.38,** it is necessarily the first one; hence, it is fronted.

But not all sentences have auxiliaries. Sometimes we have just the verb, as in these sentences:

4.44a   The windows *are* dirty.

b   *Are* the windows dirty?

4.45a   He *was* outside the office.

b   *Was* he outside the office?

4.46a   He *is* a fool.

b   *Is* he a fool?

In these sentences it is the verb—*are, was, is*—that goes before the subject, regardless of whether a predicate adjective, an adverbial, or a predicate noun follows. However, we have used forms of *be* in each sentence. What happens when we use other verbs and no auxiliary?

4.47a   They *cancelled* the concert.

b   **Cancelled* they the concert?

c   *Did* they *cancel* the concert?

4.48a   She *remembers* the combination to the safe.

b   **Remembers* she the combination to the safe?

c   *Does* she *remember* the combination to the safe?

If we had moved the verb in front of the subject, we would have derived the unsatisfactory **b** versions. At one time these were possible questions in English, but not today. Instead, we expect the **c** versions. In these questions, tense is no longer attached to the verb (*cancel, remember*), but rather to a form of *do* (*did, does*). For verbs other than *be*, then, we remove tense from the verb and attach it to *do* at the beginning of the sentence when we wish to form a question.

To summarize, we have three types of sentences in English, and we form questions in a slightly different way in each of them.

1. If the sentence contains one or more auxiliary verbs, the first one goes before the subject:

    4.49a   They *will* be leaving soon.

    b   *Will* they be leaving soon?

2. If there is no auxiliary and the main verb is *be*, move *be* before the subject:

    4.50a   The horse *is* asleep.

    b   *Is* the horse asleep?

3. If there is no auxiliary and the main verb is not *be*, detach tense from the verb and attach it to *do*, which is placed before the subject:

    4.51a   Hal *painted* the garage.

    b   *Did* Hal *paint* the garage?

In each type we move one element before the subject: the first auxiliary, *be*, or tense with *do*. It is this word order along with the intonation pattern that tells us the sentence is a question.

The questions we have examined so far are often called **yes–no questions** because of the usual responses to them. To **4.51b,** for example, we expect an answer such as "Yes, he did" or "No, he didn't" unless the other person responds with something like "I don't know" or "Would you repeat the question?" An answer such as "Tomorrow" or "Under the car" is unacceptable. Sometimes we have trouble answering a question with "Yes" or "No" even though these are the responses solicited by the person asking. "Do you still beat your wife?" and "Are zebras black or white?" are typical examples. We are irritated by questions such as these, or we laugh at them because they are so restrictively yes–no questions; neither answer is appropriate.

Sometimes we request a different type of information, such as the name of the person who performed an act, when an event occurred, and the like. We can question any part of the following sentence:

    4.52a   Anita sent the watch to Barb's daughter last week.

To ask whether the action occurred or not, we use a yes-no question:

    4.52b   Did Anita send the watch to Barb's daughter last week?

But if we want to ask about the time of the act, we form a question like this:

    4.52c   When did Anita send the watch to Barb's daughter?

The adverbial of time *last week* no longer appears in the sentence because this is what the speaker is trying to find out. Instead, the interrogative *when* takes its place, but it goes at the beginning of the sentence rather than at the end. Both **4.52b** and **4.52c** have adverbials of time: *last week* at the end of the former and *when* at the beginning of the latter. The inverted word order of tense plus *do* before the subject is found in both sentences.

    Returning to **4.52b,** we can ask about parts of the sentence other than the adverbial. For example, we can form any of the following questions:

    4.52d   What did Anita send to Barb's daughter last week?
        e   To whom did Anita send the watch last week?
        f   To whose daughter did Anita send the watch last week?
        g   Who sent the watch to Barb's daughter last week?

In each of these we have replaced a part of the sentence with a question word — *what, whom, whose, who* — and moved it to the beginning of the sentence; in **4.52e–4.52f,** we have moved the preposition *to* also. Because these sentences contain question words beginning with the letters *wh,* we call them **WH questions.** In addition to those we have examined, we can add the following:

    4.53   *Which* book did you lose?
    4.54   *Where* are you going?
    4.55   *Why* are they leaving so soon?
    4.56   *How* will you get home?
    4.57   *How many* people were at the reception?

How, of course, does not begin with *wh,* but it is convenient to retain the classification *WH question* because all the other words in this group do begin with these letters.

    Since WH questions upset the normal word order of sentences, some people have trouble deciding which word is subject, which one direct object, and so on. It is useful to consider the answer that might be given to such sentences. For example:

    4.58a   *Where* are Andrew's shoes?

b Andrew's shoes are *in the closet.*

In **4.58b,** we have no trouble recognizing *Andrew's shoes* as the subject, *are* as the verb, and *in the closet* as an adverbial of place. Even though the question **4.58a** has the reverse order (Adverbial-Verb-Subject), if we consider the answer, we readily recognize the sentence elements. Let us try this procedure with a few additional sentences:

4.59a *Why* did you make fresh coffee?

b I made fresh coffee *because we need it for lunch.*

4.60a *How* should we treat that cat?

b We should treat that cat *lovingly.*

4.61a *When* is she leaving for Alaska?

b She is leaving for Alaska *next Friday.*

In **4.59,** we clearly see that *why* is an adverbial of reason; in **4.60** *how* is manner; and in **4.61** *when* is time.

In formal usage *who* is the form used for subjects and predicate nouns, *whom* the one for objects. Yet we often substitute another pattern: *who* before the verb and *whom* after it or after a preposition. Hence, we feel comfortable with the **a** versions of the following sentences because of this position in relation to the verb:

4.62a Who pinched me?

b *Whom pinched me?

4.63a You gave it to whom?

b *You gave it to who?

4.64a Who kissed whom?

b *Whom kissed who?

With the personal pronouns (*he, she, we,* and so on), the position before the verb is almost always that of the subject, and that after the verb is frequently the direct object. However, with questions this normal word order of Subject-Verb-Object is disrupted so that we may find the object first, then part of the auxiliary, then the subject, and so on:

4.65a Harry has thanked Gloria.

b Whom has Harry thanked?

In informal English — conversation with friends, personal letters, notes, and the like — many people use *who* when it comes before the verb, regardless of how it functions in the sentence. Instead of **4.65b,** they would say,

4.65c   Who has Harry thanked?

even though they might use *whom* as in **4.65b** on more formal occasions.

In formal usage, it is necessary for us to ask how the pronoun functions, not where it occurs in relation to the verb. Except in echo questions (*You saw whom?*), interrogative pronouns come before the verb, regardless of how they are used. As with the interrogative adverbs, we can easily determine the function of pronouns by considering possible answers to the questions:

4.66a   *Who* wrote that disgusting letter?

  b   *Connie* wrote that disgusting letter. (subject)

4.67a   *Who* are they?

  b   They are *the Thompson children*. (predicate noun)

4.68a   *Whom* will she send to the convention?

  b   She will send *you* to the convention. (direct object)

4.69a   With *whom* are you arguing?

  b   I am arguing with *Travis*. (object of a preposition)

4.70a   *Whom* did he sit beside?

  b   He sat beside *Arthur*. (object of a preposition)

In the last sentence the preposition is left at the end, a practice that is sometimes discouraged in formal writing. Some people would, therefore, object to **4.70a,** preferring either of these:

4.70c   Beside whom did he sit?

  d   Who did he sit beside?

That is, both *whom* and the preposed preposition belong to formal style, and *who* as an object and the final preposition are informal. The **a** version mixes styles, whereas **c** and **d** are more consistent.

When we place the interrogative word at the beginning of the sentence, we do two things: First, we indicate to the listener or reader that the sentence is a question; second, we give prominence to the most important element by placing it first.

THE EXPLETIVE THERE

Another common type of sentence in which normal word order is disrupted is the following:

4.71   There are some quarters in the drawer.

The word *there* in this sentence is not an adverb of place, as it is in the following:

> **4.72**   *There* goes the last bus.

Rather, in **4.71** *there* has no real meaning and serves only as a filler in the subject position. We lose nothing if we omit it:

> **4.73**   Some quarters are in the drawer.

The difference between **4.71** and **4.73** is whether we wish to emphasize the existence of the quarters or not. *There* in **4.71** is called an ***expletive;*** it does not act as a modifier, a subject, or any other function.

To form sentences with the expletive *there,* we invert the subject and the verb *be* and add *there* at the beginning:

> **4.74a**   A wasp is in the room.
>   **b**   There is a wasp in the room.
> **4.75a**   Someone is at the door.
>   **b**   There is someone at the door.
> **4.76a**   Many people were at the convention.
>   **b**   There were many people at the convention.

Occasionally we can use verbs other than *be* with the expletive *there:*

> **4.77**   There will come a time when you will regret that.
> **4.78**   Once upon a time there lived a beautiful princess in a far-off kingdom.

However, such cases are rare, as we can see from the following:

> **4.79a**   Wild flowers grew in the garden.
>   **b**   *There grew wild flowers in the garden.
> **4.80a**   A welder coughed near me.
>   **b**   *There coughed a welder near me.

The usual verb with the expletive *there* is *be.*

Following *be* we normally find an adverbial of place, as in all the above examples, but sometimes we see an adjective plus a modifier:

> **4.81a**   Something is wrong with this report.
>   **b**   There is something wrong with this report.
> **4.82a**   Many people were sick with the flu.
>   **b**   There were many people sick with the flu.

Since the subject follows the verb in sentences with the expletive *there,* some people at times find the matter of subject–verb agreement confusing. A safe guide is to recast the sentence without *there:*

4.83a   There's a fly in my soup.

   b   A fly is in my soup.

4.84a   There are two flies in my soup.

   b   Two flies are in my soup.

4.85a   There is a bathroom upstairs.

   b   A bathroom is upstairs.

4.86a   There are a bathroom and a den upstairs.

   b   A bathroom and a den are upstairs.

With the **b** versions of these sentences there is no question about what is the subject. Whereas we might hear

4.86c   There's a bathroom and a den upstairs.

we would seldom hear

4.86d   *A bathroom and a den is upstairs.

It is easier to recognize the structure in the noninverted sentences without *there.*

INDIRECT OBJECTS

We have seen that the usual place for adverbials is at the end:

4.87a   Edgar threw the ball *to Mike.*

We recognize *Edgar* as the subject, *threw* as the verb, *the ball* as the direct object, and *to Mike* as a prepositional phrase functioning as an adverbial of direction. If we moved the prepositional phrase before the direct object, the result would be awkward:

4.87b   Edgar threw *to Mike* the ball.

However, we can delete the preposition and produce an acceptable sentence:

4.87c   Edgar threw *Mike* the ball.

Mike now is a complement known as an **indirect object.** The traditional definition of the indirect object as the one to whom or for whom the action is performed is usually fairly accurate.

Here are some more examples in which prepositional phrases are moved and converted into indirect objects:

4.88a   The Dean wrote a letter *to the student*.

   b   The Dean wrote *the student* a letter.

4.89a   The chef baked a birthday cake *for Ben*.

   b   The chef baked *Ben* a birthday cake.

The indirect object usually names a human or an animal, but a few verbs such as *give* may take inanimate indirect objects:

4.90   We gave *the wall* a fresh coat of paint.

We saw that direct objects occur with transitive verbs. Indirect objects occur with a small subclass of these verbs. Most common are certain verbs of motion: *throw, toss, send, pitch, give,* and the like. They also occur with such verbs as *bake, make, cook, build, pass,* and *bring*.

When a verb has both an indirect and a direct object, it is word order that signals the relationship: Subject–Verb–Indirect Object–Direct Object:

4.91   Your grandmother left you a message.

A sentence is seldom incomplete without an indirect object:

4.92a   Mr. Chapman wired me the money.

   b   Mr. Chapman wired the money.

4.93a   They gave us their old clothes.

   b   They gave their old clothes.

4.94a   Janet's mother bought her a new dress.

   b   Janet's mother bought a new dress.

Without the indirect object, the sentences are less exact. If we try deleting the direct object, we run into problems:

4.92c   Mr. Chapman wired me.

4.93c   They gave us.

4.94c   Janet's mother bought her.

These sentences are not just less exact than the **a** versions; they have different meanings. The direct object is more basic than the indirect object.

A few verbs such as *ask* and *teach* permit deletion of either object:

4.95a   The driver asked me the time.

   b   The driver asked the time.

   c   The driver asked me.

Some grammarians have said that these verbs take two direct objects; however, the semantic relationships are not the same for both objects, and the word order suggests that the first is an indirect object. With *teach* the first object can be paraphrased with a *to* phrase, and some sentences with *ask* can be paraphrased with *of.* It seems reasonable to say that deletion with these verbs is exceptional; otherwise they are like other verbs that permit indirect objects.

WORD ORDER IN POETRY

In addition to the types of variation we have examined in the preceding sections, we often find orderings of words in poetry that differ from those which we would expect in contemporary prose. In most instances these variants are survivals of orders that were once common in English but have since become archaic. For example, our present pattern of Subject-Verb-Complement has always been the basic one in English, but minor patterns could also be found in early times. In Old English, the language before about 1100 A.D., noun objects usually followed the verb as they do today, but pronoun objects normally preceded it, giving the order Subject-Pronoun Object-Verb (e.g., *John him hit* instead of *John hit him*). Even noun objects could occur between the subject and the verb (*Linda the water drank*), but this was a less common ordering than Subject-Verb-Noun Object (*Linda drank the water*).

By the beginning of the Modern English period (around 1500), the ordering Subject-Verb-Object had become well established in prose, but poetry often did not conform, as in Sonnet 31 of Sidney's *Astrophel and Stella:*

> What, may it be that even in heavenly place
> That busy archer his sharp arrows tries?

Instead of the expected "That busy archer [Cupid] tries his sharp arrows," we have both the subject and the object preceding the verb. We know that *that busy archer* is the subject of *tries* because of the singular form of the verb; with a plural subject such as *arrows,* the verb would have been *try.* We also know that this meaning of *try* normally has an animate subject; *archer* fits, but *arrows* does not.

Here are two other examples in which the usual word order is not observed:

> A little bread shall do me stead,
> Much bread I not desire.

In the second line the object precedes the subject; the expected order would be "I do not desire much bread." For the second example:

A broken altar, Lord, thy servant rears,
Made of a heart, and cemented with tears:

Again, the object (*a broken altar*) and the subject (*thy servant*) both occur before the verb. In the Sidney sonnet the subject precedes the object; here it is the other way around. The reader has to recognize the syntactic relationship if the lines are to have meaning.

It should not be assumed that poets have complete freedom in their arrangements of words. If they did, providing metrically regular lines that rime would be simple, as would providing or avoiding alliteration, assonance, and other patterns. For most poetry, the word order is scarcely different from that of prose. When poets decide to vary this order, they do so with definite restrictions, usually limiting themselves to patterns that were once widespread but that have since become archaic. For poetry, the reader has to be able to grasp the syntactic structures to understand the meaning; if poets had unlimited freedom, no one would understand them.

EXERCISES

A. After each of the following statements are two questions, one of which corresponds to the statement and one that does not. For the latter explain how the statement and question differ (e.g., present tense in one and past in the other, the progressive *be* in one but not in the other, etc.).

  1a. They could hear him in the next room.
   b. Could they hear him in the next room?
   c. Can they hear him in the next room?
  2a. Ann has been washing her hair.
   b. Has Ann been washing her hair?
   c. Has Ann washed her hair?
  3a. The barn burned.
   b. Has the barn burned?
   c. Did the barn burn?
  4a. He knew the way home.
   b. Did he know the way home?
   c. Does he know the way home?

B. Explain why the **b** versions are not possible in standard English:

1a. May Hal go with us?
 b. *May go Hal with us?
2a. Do you believe that story?
 b. *Believe you that story?
3a. Has she been calling us?
 b. *Has been she calling us?
4a. Were you at school today?
 b. *Did you be at school today?
5a. Did the program last long?
 b. *Did the program lasted long?

C. Convert the following statements into yes–no questions:

 1. Gerald has stepped on the orange.
 2. We must tolerate rudeness.
 3. The Robinsons were at the beach.
 4. She called at midnight.
 5. Helen is poking fun at her niece.
 6. You believe in Santa Claus.
 7. They are courageous.
 8. Adeline has been brushing her hair.
 9. Someone grabbed her arm.
 10. They could have been there.

D. Convert the following sentences into WH questions by replacing the italicized words with the appropriate interrogative pronoun or adverb:

 1. Beverly invited *Joe Randolph* to her party.
 2. You were standing *in front of the drugstore* at six o'clock.
 3. *You* drew this insulting picture of me.
 4. Connie will finish the report *soon*.
 5. Everyone has been staring at Kathryn *because she has choco- late on her chin*.
 6. Everett had sat behind *Art* all semester.
 7. We should thank *Mr. Kelly*.
 8. You gave the position to *Jeff*.
 9. She walks *with a limp* now.
 10. He has become *a baker*.

E. Provide full-sentence answers for the following questions, replacing the interrogative pronouns and adverbs with specific words and changing *you* to *I* (or vice versa) when necessary. Then give the function of each interrogative (subject, direct object, adverbial of time, etc.).

1. Where did I leave my umbrella?
2. Near whom are you building your new house?
3. What will they eat?
4. Who has been smoking in here?
5. Whom did she ride with to the picnic?
6. Why are you laughing at me?
7. When shall we three meet again?
8. Which shoes do you prefer?
9. What could Allan draw on the blackboard?
10. How does the patient seem to you?
11. How are they getting along?
12. Whose pen is this?
13. Who are they?
14. How are you?
15. To whom will you leave your rings?
16. Where has he been hiding all this time?
17. Whom will you show your drawing?
18. Whom did she call?
19. Whom are you mocking?
20. Who sneezed?

F. Write two answers for each of the following questions, one with an adverbial of manner and a second with a verb that conveys the meaning of the adverbial. You may use slang if it is vivid.

example: How did they go into the room?
          They went into the room slowly.
          They crept into the room.

1. How will you drink the Coke?
2. How should we leave the party?
3. How is she commenting on the movie?
4. How have they spent their money?
5. How did you move to the chair?
6. How have the prices been going?
7. How would Mike call to his brother?
8. How did you write the note?
9. How is he removing his shoes?
10. How had Cathy run down the street?

G. Rewrite the following lines of poetry so that they follow normal word order:

1. Blue were her eyes as the fairy-flax,
   Her cheeks like the dawn of day.
   [Longfellow, "The Wreck of the Hesperus"]

2. The skipper, he blew a whiff from his pipe,
   And a scornful laugh laughed he.
   [*Ibid.*]
3. Colder and louder blew the wind,
   A gale from the Northeast,
   [*Ibid.*]
4. Spring, the sweet spring, is the year's pleasant king,
   Then blooms each thing, then maids dance in a ring,
   [Nashe, "Spring, the Sweet Spring"]
5. My sweetest Lesbia, let us live and love,
   And though the sager sort our deeds reprove,
   Let us not weigh them.
   [Campion, "My Sweetest Lesbia"]
6. I have seen roses damasked, red and white,
   But no such roses see I in her cheeks;
   [Shakespeare, Sonnet 130]
7. Much have I traveled in the realms of gold,
   And many goodly states and kingdoms seen;
   [Keats, "On First Looking into Chapman's Homer"]
8. Here will I sit and wait,
   While to my ear from uplands far away
   The bleating of the folded flocks is borne,
   [Arnold, "The Scholar Gypsy"]
9. On either side the river lie
   Long fields of barley and of rye,
   [Tennyson, "The Lady of Shalott"]
10. There lived a wife at Usher's Well,
    And a wealthy wife was she;
    ["The Wife of Usher's Well"]

5

Passives

Although normal word order is SVO, we sometimes vary this arrangement to form questions, to emphasize certain words, or to provide variety. One means of giving prominence to a word is to place it first in the sentence:

> **5.1** *Yesterday* he was all right.

We sometimes move objects to the beginning, just as we do adverbials:

> **5.2** *That* you must never do again!
>
> **5.3** *This one* I especially like.

These fronted objects have extra stress placed on them when the sentences are spoken.

PASSIVES WITH BE

At times we cannot move the object to the beginning of the sentence:

> **5.4** Audrey chose Peter.

If we fronted the object as we did in **5.2** and **5.3,** we would obtain the unacceptable:

> **5.5** *Peter Audrey chose.

Yet we do have a structure known as the *passive* that permits us to place the receiver of the action first:

> **5.6**   Peter was chosen by Audrey.

We understand this sentence to mean the same as the **active 5.4,** namely that Audrey did the choosing and that Peter was the one chosen.

Let us see how we revised **5.4** to produce **5.6,** both repeated here:

> **5.4**   Audrey chose Peter.
> **5.6**   Peter was chosen by Audrey.

First of all, the nouns have been interchanged. The one that occurs before the verb in **5.4** (*Audrey*) is after it in **5.6,** and the one after the verb in **5.4** (*Peter*) is in front of it in **5.6.** If we switch the nouns in **5.4,** we derive the following:

> **5.7**   Peter   chose   Audrey.

But this by itself is not what we want because it yields the wrong meaning. We notice next that *by* appears in the passive sentence. Let us place it before *Audrey:*

> **5.8**   Peter   chose   by Audrey.

This is still not enough to produce a passive sentence. We must do something to the verb. We may ask what is the difference between *chose* and *was chosen.* Both contain *choose,* and both sentences are in past tense. The passive also contains *was,* the past tense of *be.* Instead of the present participle that we are accustomed to seeing after the auxiliary *be* (*He was choosing*), we find the past participle, *was chosen.* Now if we add *be* and make the word after it a past participle, we can change **5.8** into the following:

> **5.9**   Peter   was chosen   by Audrey.

This sentence is what we are trying to produce.

Let us go through the steps for forming the passive with another sentence:

> **5.10**   The rat ate the cheese.

First we interchange the noun phrases:

> **5.11**   The cheese   ate   the rat.

Next we insert *by:*

    5.12   The cheese   ate   by the rat.

Finally we add *be* and make the main verb a past participle:

    5.13   The cheese   was eaten   by the rat.

We recognize this sentence as synonymous with the active sentence **5.10**. In both, the rat did the eating and the cheese is that which was eaten.

So far we have seen only sentences with a main verb and no auxiliaries. We now should consider the position of the passive *be* when other auxiliaries are present.

    5.14a   The director has forgotten the letter.

       b   The letter has been forgotten by the director.

As we can see, the passive *be* follows the auxiliary *have*. Here are some examples with other auxiliaries:

    5.15a   The valedictorian should deliver the address.

       b   The address should be delivered by the valedictorian.

    5.16a   The nurse was bathing the baby.

       b   The baby was being bathed by the nurse.

    5.17a   An imbecile must have written this letter.

       b   This letter must have been written by an imbecile.

In each pair of sentences we see the noun phrases interchanged and *by* added in the passive versions. The passive *be* follows all other auxiliaries, and the word after it is a past participle (*delivered, bathed, written*). The form of the passive *be* is determined in each case by the auxiliary that precedes it: the infinitive *be* after a modal (**5.15**), the present participle *being* after *be* (**5.16**), and the past participle *been* (**5.17**) after *have*. Notice that both active and passive versions have the same meaning, including that provided by the auxiliaries. If one is progressive, so is the other, and so on.

Although many combinations of auxiliaries are possible in the passive, a few are not, namely those combinations of the progressive *be* preceded by *have* or a modal:

    5.18a   The dog has been chasing Michael.

       b   *Michael has been being chased by the dog.

    5.19a   The owners should be washing the windows.

       b   *The windows should be being washed by the owners.

    5.20a   That man must have been watching our house.

       b   *Our house must have been being watched by that man.

Other combinations of auxiliaries occur freely in the passive, as we saw in **5.14–5.17.**

Only sentences with direct objects may be converted into passives. Hence, there is no passive for sentences with intransitive verbs:

5.21a   The smoke vanished.

b   *Was vanished by the smoke.

5.22a   The noise is subsiding.

b   *Is being subsided by the noise.

Nor do sentences with predicate nouns become passives:

5.23a   Al has become a nuisance.

b   *A nuisance has been become by Al.

5.24a   The guest of honor remained my bridge partner.

b   *My bridge partner was remained by the guest of honor.

The **b** versions of **5.21–5.24** are so bad it is obvious that only sentences with direct objects may become passives.

In addition, there is a small list of verbs that do not form passives, as illustrated by the following examples:

5.25a   This weather suits me.

b   *I am suited by this weather.

5.26a   The record album cost $5.95.

b   *$5.95 was cost by the record album.

Other verbs that normally block the passive are *have, weigh, measure, resemble, involve, marry, total, owe, possess, include, form, want, fit, suit,* and perhaps a few more. Some of the verbs have more than one meaning:

5.27a   Someone stupid must have weighed that package.

5.28a   The package must have weighed ten pounds.

In **5.27a,** *weigh* names an action, but in **5.28a** it names a state. Let us see how the two uses behave in the passive:

5.27b   That package must have been weighed by someone stupid.

5.28b   *Ten pounds must have been weighed by the package.

The action verb *weigh* does not block the passive, but the stative verb does.

In addition to some verbs that have only active versions, such as the statives in the preceding paragraph, there are a few that have only passive forms:

5.29 It was *rumored* that he had been found.

5.30 They are *alleged* to have been witnesses.

5.31 Janice was *born* in Montreal.

It is pointless to try to provide active counterparts for these sentences.

At times the subject in the active sentence is an indefinite pronoun, as in the following:

5.32a Someone has stabbed the barber.

b The barber has been stabbed by someone.

We usually delete the *by* phrase in passives such as this, giving:

5.32c The barber has been stabbed.

We no longer have the *by* phrase to mark the sentence as a passive, but we do have *be* plus a past participle (*stabbed*). Here are some other examples of deleted *by* phrases:

5.33a Something is mashing me.

b I'm being mashed by something.

c I'm being mashed.

5.34a Someone pushed him.

b He was pushed by someone.

c He was pushed.

If the subject of the active sentence is not an indefinite pronoun such as *someone* or *something,* it usually cannot be deleted:

5.35a Randy pushed him.

b He was pushed by Randy.

If we deleted *by Randy,* we would lose information. We understand *He was pushed* to be equivalent to *He was pushed by someone,* as in **5.34.**

There is one other case in which the *by* phrase may be deleted — when the meaning of the verb is such that only one performer of the action is likely:

5.36a The jury found the defendant guilty.

b The defendant was found guilty by the jury.

c The defendant was found guilty.

5.37a A policeman has arrested Rhoda.

b Rhoda has been arrested by a policeman.

c Rhoda has been arrested.

It is only in sentences such as these that a noun phrase other than an indefinite pronoun may be deleted.

PAST PARTICIPLES AND ADJECTIVES

Some sentences admit two separate readings, depending upon how we interpret the word following *be:*

> **5.38** The door was closed.

This sentence may describe an action or a state. If we add other words after *closed* or compare the sentence with its opposite with *open/ opened,* the ambiguity becomes obvious. When we talk about an action, we are free to add manner adverbials:

> **5.39** The door was closed suddenly.

> **5.40** The door was opened suddenly.

With the stative meaning we can use an adverbial of duration:

> **5.41** The door was closed throughout the performance.

> **5.42** The door was open throughout the performance.

Although some people consider both **5.39** and **5.41** passive sentences, there are two problems with such a classification. First, if **5.41** is a passive, it seems that **5.42** should be also; yet *open* is clearly an adjective, not a past participle. Apart from the *-ed* ending on *closed* and our knowledge that it is etymologically related to the verb *close,* there is no reason to consider **5.41** a passive; in fact, it is closer to **5.42** than to **5.39**. Second, if **5.41** is a passive, it must have a deleted *by* phrase and a corresponding active version, yet neither of the following is possible:

> **5.43a** *The door was closed throughout the performance by someone.

> **b** *Someone closed the door throughout the performance.

Instead of calling *closed* in **5.41** a past participle, we will call it an adjective, the same as *open.* Its resemblance to the passive verb phrase *was closed* is a matter of etymological interest only.

To recapitulate, let us look at *broken:*

> **5.44a** The window was broken.

> **b** The window was broken all winter.

> **c** The window was broken intentionally.

The **a** version is ambiguous; the other two are not, **b** naming a state and **c** an action. If we consider **b** a sentence with a linking verb and a predicate adjective (*broken*), we can account for the absence of the following:

> **5.44d** *The window was broken by hail all winter.

> **e** *Hail broke the window all winter.

Since **5.44b** is not a passive, there is no reason to expect the **d** and **e** versions. We could substitute an adjective such as *dirty* for *broken* in this sentence and have the same structure. On the other hand, **c** is a passive, and we do have a corresponding active:

    5.44f   Someone broke the window intentionally.

By calling *broken* an adjective in **5.44b** and a past participle in **5.44c,** we can account for the ambiguity of **5.44a.**

PASSIVES WITH GET

In addition to passives formed with the auxiliary *be,* there are those formed with *get:*

    5.45a   Something bit John.
       b   John was bitten.
       c   John got bitten.

The passive with *get* occurs frequently in spoken English and in some informal writing, but it is rarely found in formal writing.

    Like *be, get* can also be a linking verb:

    5.46   Caleb was sick.
    5.47   Caleb got sick.

The meaning of *get* in **5.47** is very close to that of *become.* There are also several additional meanings of *get,* as we can see from the following examples:

    5.48   They got to worrying about it.
    5.49   They have got to go.
    5.50   They've got a new car.
    5.51   They got up.
    5.52   They got the message.
    5.53   He got his nose out of joint.

We will be concerned only with the passive meaning.

    Because *get* has more meaning than *be* in some uses, such as **5.48–5.53,** there is a tendency to expect a difference in meaning between passives with *be* and those with *get.* In some sentences we may see such a difference:

    5.54   Cathy was arrested.
    5.55   Cathy got arrested.

We feel in **5.55** that Cathy was in some way responsible for the arrest; that is, it has the following meaning:

> **5.56**   Cathy got herself arrested.

Passives with *be* do not permit reflexives such as *herself:*

> **5.57**   *Cathy was herself arrested.

It would be tempting to say that passives with *be* make no statements about responsibility, but those with *get* do. However, such a generalization would be inaccurate because passives with *get* usually have two meanings, one with and the other without indications of responsibility:

> **5.58a**   Cathy got arrested through no fault of her own.
> **5.59a**   Cathy got arrested on purpose.

Note that **5.59** permits the insertion of *herself*, but **5.58** does not:

> **5.58b**   *Cathy got herself arrested through no fault of her own.
> **5.59b**   Cathy got herself arrested on purpose.

Whenever resonsibility on the part of the subject is intended, a reflexive pronoun (*herself, themselves, myself,* etc.) is either expressed or understood.

In some sentences the meaning with the reflexive is unlikely but remotely possible:

> **5.60a**   I got caught in traffic.
> **b**   ?I got myself caught in traffic.
> **5.61a**   We got rained on.
> **b**   ?We got ourselves rained on.
> **5.62a**   Eloise finally got paid.
> **b**   ?Eloise finally got herself paid.

The question mark means that we did not want to indicate that the **b** sentences are impossible (although **5.62b** may be), as would be the case if we had used an asterisk; yet we wanted to show that they are questionable.

We can, therefore, state the difference in meaning between passives with *be* and those with *get* as follows: Those with *be* make no statement about whether the subject is responsible for the action or not. Passives with *get* are ambiguous, having either the same neutral meaning as those with *be* or implying responsibility on the part of the subject. This ambiguity may be removed with the use of a relfexive pronoun or with certain adverbials (e.g., *through no fault of her own*).

Turning from meaning to form, we see that both passive auxiliaries are followed by past participles:

5.63 Herbert was *chosen.*

5.64 Herbert got *chosen.*

Also, both follow all other auxiliaries:

5.65 You might have *been* killed.

5.66 You might have *got* killed.

Yet there are some differences. First of all, adverbs are not positioned in the same place with the two passive auxiliaries:

5.67a We finally were noticed.

b We were finally noticed.

5.68a We finally got noticed.

b *We got finally noticed.

Some people may have stylistic preferences for positioning adverbs with *be,* choosing **5.67a** or **5.67b;** however, there is no freedom with *get.*

Second, in questions *be* is moved before the subject if it is the first auxiliary:

5.69a They were erased.

b Were they erased?

Questions with *get* are formed in the same manner as those with verbs other than *be:*

5.70a They got erased.

b *Got they erased?

c Did they get erased?

The same pattern can be found with negatives:

5.71a They were erased.

b They were not erased.

Not follows *be.* With other verbs, *do* support is required:

5.72a Sheila sneezed.

b *Sheila sneezed not.

c Sheila didn't sneeze.

Passives with *get* form negatives in the same way:

5.73a They got erased.

b *They got not erased.

c They didn't get erased.

With questions, negatives, and similar structures, then, the passive auxiliary *get* does not function like *be,* but rather like other verbs.

WHY USE THE PASSIVE?

Grammar texts frequently caution students against using the passive, saying that it is less direct than the active and citing examples such as the following:

    5.74a   The book was read by me.

    5.75a   A good time was had by everyone.

These sentences would clearly be better as actives:

    5.74b   I read the book.

    5.75b   Everyone had a good time.

Examples such as these are unfortunate because they represent only restricted types of passives, not the full range. In particular, when the subject of an active sentence is a first-person pronoun (*I, we*), passives are rarely acceptable unless heavy stress is placed on the object of *by:*

    5.76   The wall was painted by *us,* not by *them.*

Sentence **5.74a** is objectionable not just because it is a passive, but because it belongs to the subclass in which the object of *by* is *me* or *us.* Similarly, **5.75a** is unfortunate because it is trite and because this is one of the few instances in which *have* permits a passive; it normally functions like *weigh, measure,* and other stative verbs that we discussed earlier in this chapter.

When we examine books and articles written by distinguished authors, we do not find sentences like **5.74a** and **5.75a,** but we do find certain types of passives used rather frequently. In the majority of cases these sentences have the *by* phrase deleted. Why, then, do writers use the passive and suppress this noun or pronoun? First, the use of *someone* or *something* seems wordy:

    5.77a   Someone has stolen my car.

       b   My car has been stolen.

If the car has been stolen, it is obvious that someone took it.

Second, by placing *my car* first in **5.77b,** we are giving prominence to it rather than to *someone.* We may be concerned that the thief be found and sent to prison, but our main interest when we state the sentence is with the car, not with the unknown, faceless thief.

Third, we may be intentionally suppressing information:

    5.78a   I was told that you are getting a divorce.

We could have used an active sentence with *someone:*

    5.78b   Someone told me that you are getting a divorce.

But we would then be emphasizing our reluctance to divulge our source.

Fourth, we may wish to be tactful and suppress the name of the responsible person:

    5.79a You made a mistake in my bill.

       b Someone made a mistake in my bill.

       c A mistake was made in my bill.

The passive version is more polite than either of the other two, especially if we know we are writing or speaking to the guilty person.

Fifth, in scientific and some other kinds of scholarly writing, authors may want to provide a greater degree of objectivity than would be possible with specific subjects, especially when referring to themselves or to their colleagues:

    5.80a We have proved that ...

       b It has been proved that ...

    5.81a I believe that ...

       b It is believed that ...

The origin of the belief or proof is not given.

Finally, some indefinite pronouns are objectionable for stylistic reasons:

    5.82a One can find zebras in Africa.

       b You can find zebras in Africa.

       c Zebras can be found in Africa.

The first version with *one* sounds stiff to many people, and the second sentence with the indefinite *you* is generally not acceptable in formal writing. The passive version avoids both problems.

EXERCISES

A. The **b** sentences below are intended as passive counterparts of the **a** sentences, but some are unsatisfactory because a change other than that needed to form the passive was made. Locate the passives that are incorrect, explain what is wrong, and correct them.

    1a. The attendant has already parked your car.

      b. Your car had already been parked by the attendant.

    2a. An odious person was whistling a patriotic tune.

      b. A patriotic tune was whistled by an odious person.

3a. Janice must have noticed the dripping faucet.
 b. The dripping faucet must have been noticed by Janice.
4a. The dog was digging a hole.
 b. A hole was being dug by the dog.
5a. The passengers could hear the pilot's announcement.
 b. The pilot's announcement could have been heard by the passengers.

B. Convert the following sentences into passives, deleting the *by* phrase wherever possible:

1. Someone has found a bomb in the basement.
2. People can't trust him.
3. Olivia drove the bus.
4. Someone must have found him by now.
5. The referee was attacking Gwendolyn.
6. The auditor has carefully audited your account.
7. The judge pronounced the sentence.
8. Judge Bates pronounced the sentence.
9. Someone has called the wrong number.
10. Her parents reared her in South America.

C. Some words can be either adjectives or past participles, such as *closed* and *broken*. Others are only one of these. Create sentences like *The door was closed* for the following words and classify them as: (1) either participle or adjective, (2) only participle, or (3) only adjective.

1. embarrassed	6. shut	11. disheveled
2. elated	7. amazed	12. amused
3. paid	8. married	13. degraded
4. inspired	9. caught	14. stricken
5. named	10. concerned	15. dedicated

Add ten additional words and follow the same directions.

D. Convert the active sentences to passives and the passives to actives. Delete the *by* phrase in the passive whenever possible. Decide which version is better in each case and try to explain why.

1. Albert loves Wanda.
2. Hank must have been questioned by the teacher.
3. The building is cooled by central air conditioning.
4. Lightning struck the tree.
5. The window was closed by me.
6. Someone left the lights on all night.

7. The detective got shot.
8. Barbara could smell the cabbage.
9. You've been had.
10. Evelyn got caught by the teacher.
11. Someone must clean everything today.
12. That book can be found on the third level of the stacks.
13. This acrobatic team is admired all over the world.
14. I was reared in New England.
15. The window washer saw a strange sight.
16. In 1945 the allied powers defeated Germany.
17. Everyone signed the birthday card.
18. She was obsessed by a strange notion.
19. Tony wrote a poem.
20. The piano tuner tuned the piano today.

E. Draw a chart with four columns: Subject, Verb, Complement, and Adverbial. Then write the words from the following sentences in the proper columns and classify the complements and adverbials.

1. The salespeople were watching the customer.
2. He got nasty after his sixteenth drink.
3. Brenda felt ashamed.
4. I painted all morning.
5. His friends were broken-hearted.
6. My glasses got broken.
7. His arm was bent at the elbow.
8. Her card was bent accidentally.
9. The plant grew fast last year.
10. The plant grew tall in the greenhouse.
11. He grew tomatoes.
12. The pupil was reading aloud.
13. That story was exciting.
14. The child was exciting the animals.
15. The Andersons are divorced.
16. Carla was divorced by her husband.
17. She slept in the living room.
18. It will turn cold tonight.
19. Everything must be approached with care.
20. He was a roughneck all summer.

F. Select three passages of approximately one thousand words each and analyze the passives that you find.

1. Do you find a larger number of passives in some passages than in others? If so, what reasons do you suggest for the difference?

2. What percentage of the passives have deleted *by* phrases?
3. How many active sentences do you find with indefinite pronouns as subjects?
4. For each sentence containing a transitive verb, try to determine why the author decided to use the active or the passive.
5. What is the proportion of passives with *be* to those with *get?*

6

The Noun Phrase

As we examined sentences in the preceding chapters, we frequently mentioned noun phrases and their functions as subjects, objects, predicate nouns, and objects of prepositions:

6.1 *Those shoes* are new. (subject)

6.2 The cowboy roped *the steer*. (direct object)

6.3 Your sister is *a pest*. (predicate noun)

6.4 I sent the check to *the bank*. (object of a preposition)

The objects of certain prepositions can be converted into indirect objects:

6.5a I signaled the answer to *Bob*.

  b I signaled *Bob* the answer.

In a passive sentence we rearrange the subject and object noun phrases:

6.6a A rattlesnake bit Carolyn.

  b Carolyn was bitten by a rattlesnake.

Because it is only by its use in a sentence that we can classify a word as a noun or any other part of speech, we have devoted the first five chapters of this book to the study of functions. It is now time to look more closely at the noun phrase, the structure that performs the functions we have been discussing.

FUNCTIONS OF NOUN PHRASES

We have already mentioned the most important uses of nouns, but there are two others that we should now consider. First is the *appositive,* a noun that follows another noun and refers to the same person or thing:

> **6.7** Evelyn, *my niece,* wrote this letter.

Evelyn and *my niece* are the same person. Normally we provide our listeners or readers with only the information necessary for conveying the message. If we were speaking to people who know Evelyn, they would think it strange if we proceeded to identify her, as in **6.7;** on the other hand, if they do not know her and we have not mentioned her previously, some such identification is useful. At other times we may know two or more people with the same name; then the appositive *my niece* tells which one is intended. Sentence **6.7** is appropriate whenever we can use the following:

> **6.8** Evelyn wrote this letter. She is my niece.

If *She is my niece* is not redundant, then neither is the sentence with the appositive.

As sentences **6.7** and **6.8** show, the appositive is similar to the predicate noun in that both rename another noun. There are important differences, however. The predicate noun is separated from the noun it renames by a linking verb, but the appositive follows immediately:

> **6.9**   Mr. Richardson became *my worst enemy.* (predicate noun)
>
> **6.10** Mr. Richardson, *my worst enemy,* snubbed me. (appositive)

Another difference is that the predicate noun always renames the subject, whereas the appositive can rename any noun in the sentence:

> **6.11** Mr. Smith, *my teacher,* left this. (renames the subject)
>
> **6.12** He hit Earl, *Charlie's brother.* (renames the direct object)

6.13 That woman is my neighbor, *Mrs. Reece.* (renames the predicate noun)

6.14 He was talking to the coach, *an old bore.* (renames the object of a preposition)

Although the appositive and the predicate noun provide similar information, we make a distinction between them.

Let us now turn to another function of nouns and adjectives: the **objective complement.** Just as the predicate noun and predicate adjective rename or describe the subject, there are words that refer to the object:

6.15 We consider him *a fool.*

6.16 We consider him *lucky.*

6.17 They named the baby *Carolyn.*

6.18 She dyed her hair *green.*

In many sentences, such as **6.15** and **6.16,** we understand *to be* between the direct object and the objective complement:

6.19 We consider him to be a fool.

6.20 We consider him to be lucky.

For other sentences, such as **6.17** and **6.18,** no such words are understood. Whenever *to be* is understood, it helps us to distinguish between objective complements and appositives.

As we have seen before, it is the class of the verb that determines which complements follow. Linking verbs are followed by predicate nouns or adjectives. Transitive verbs take direct objects, and a small subclass of these take objective complements. Some of these permit both noun and adjective complements. such as *consider* in **6.15** and **6.16.** Others, like *name* (**6.17**), take only noun objective complements, and those like *dye* (**6.18**) take only adjectives.

In many sentences we may omit the objective complement and still have a complete sentence:

6.21a The members elected Allan president.

b The members elected Allan.

6.22a We painted the box yellow.

b We painted the box.

The direct object, however, may not be omitted:

6.21c *The members elected president.

6.22c *We painted yellow.

Usually the omission of the objective complement reduces the meaning of the sentence but does not affect its acceptability; however, we must retain the direct object.

Occasionally a sentence with an objective complement looks like one with an indirect object, as the old joke "Call me a taxi" illustrates. The comedian who delivers the line intends *me* as an indirect object and *taxi* as a direct object, as in the paraphrase "Call a taxi for me." The partner misunderstands the sentence and treats *me* as a direct object and *a taxi* as an objective complement and replies, "All right, you're a taxi."

With the appositive and the objective complement, we have considered all the uses of noun phrases that will be found in this book. Let us review them with examples:

    6.23   *The cat* purred. (subject)

    6.24   We wrote *the letter.* (direct object)

    6.25   You are *a real jewel.* (predicate noun)

    6.26   Your partner, *a real jewel,* is stupid. (appositive)

    6.27   She called me *a liar.* (objective complement)

    6.28   She gave *Tim* a piece of cake. (indirect object)

    6.29   The shoe is under *the bed.* (object of a preposition)

Since there are several complements that appear next to each other, let us see how we can distinguish them:

    6.30   We called her son, Carl.

    6.31   We called her son Carl.

    6.32   We gave Carl a dollar.

In **6.30,** *her son* is a direct object and *Carl* is an appositive. We could have interchanged them (*We called Carl, her son*) without affecting the meaning; we could also have omitted the appositive (*We called her son*). Sentence **6.31,** however, means something like "We used the name *Carl* when speaking to or about her son, even though his name was really Phil." We could not interchange the two complements without affecting the meaning. Finally, in **6.32** *Carl* is an indirect object and *a dollar* a direct object, as we can see from the paraphrase "We gave a dollar to Carl." We notice that indirect and direct objects refer to different people or things, whereas direct objects and objective complements refer to the same ones.

UNIQUE NOUNS AND NAMES OF CLASSES

We can speak or write about specific items or about members of classes. One means of doing this is to use a ***proper noun*** to name a specific person or place and a ***common noun*** for a class. For example, the

common noun *country* applies to several hundred national units; if we
wish to designate one member of this class, we use a proper noun such
as *Germany, Nigeria, Peru, Mexico, India,* or *Japan.* We can list a few
other examples:

Common Noun	*Proper Nouns*
city	Rome, Istanbul, Sidney, Cairo, Caracas
county	Kent, Washtenaw, Marin, Yoknapatawpha
university	Oxford, Sorbonne, Stanford, Princeton
planet	Mars, Jupiter, Mercury, Saturn
river	Seine, Amazon, Yangtze, Guadalquivir
state	Vermont, Ohio, Tennessee, Utah
woman	Beth, Ms. Hopkins, Aunt Julia

A common noun refers to a number of people or objects with similar
characteristics; a proper noun refers to one that is unique.

If we considered all people, places, and things in the world, we
would find several with the same names. There are probably thousands
of males named *Robert,* and some names of cities are not restricted to
one location (e.g., *Springfield, Portland, New London, San Juan*). Yet
the context is usually such that only one person or place is likely. If the
mother of a boy named Robert asks her husband, "Where is Robert?"
he does not think she means Robert Redford or Robert Goulet. Nor are
people living near Springfield, Illinois, confused upon hearing that a
neighbor has "gone to Springfield for the day"; they do not think the
speaker means Springfield, Missouri. In case the meaning is not clear
from the context, we add other details, such as *Portland, Oregon.*
Names like *Robert, Portland,* and *Springfield* are proper nouns that
designate people or places unique within a given context.

Although common nouns name classes rather than individual
items, we have ways of making them designate a specific member of
the class without giving them proper names. In a restaurant we may
order "a steak," meaning any member of the class of meats called *steak.*
Once we have made the order, we are no longer concerned with just
any steak, but with a particular one. If we call the waiter back and
mention our order, we do not use sentences like the following:

6.33a   When will a steak be ready?

6.34a   I forgot to tell you that I would like a steak well done.

Once we have singled out a specific member of the class, we stop referring to it with the article *a* or *an* and switch to *the:*

6.33b   When will the steak be ready?

6.34b   I forgot to tell you that I would like the steak well done.

As long as we mean any member of the class, we continue using *a* or *an;* to designate a specific one that has been identified, we use *the*.

At times shared knowledge permits us to use *the* on the first mentioning of an object. For example, joint owners of a car would understand

6.35   Are you taking the car?

Also, under specific circumstances, the following would be clear:

6.36   Have you seen the play yet?

6.37   Where did the batter go?

6.38   What happened to the radio?

Since we know how many suns are visible from the earth and how many devils certain religions recognize, we may say the following:

6.39   The sun rose at 6:45 this morning.

6.40   He is not afraid of the devil.

These words are still common nouns, but they are specifically identified with *the*.

The usual term for *a* is **indefinite article,** and that for *the* is **definite article.** There are also **demonstratives,** which indicate a definite object just as *the* does. They also provide additional information, as we can see from these examples:

6.41   *This* tulip came from Holland.

6.42   *These* apples are rotten.

6.43   I like *that* song.

6.44   She handed *those* children the passes.

Although we do not necessarily point our fingers or nod our heads at the objects named when we use the demonstratives, we do so mentally. As we can tell from the examples, *this* and its plural *these* are used for objects that are near; *that* and the plural *those* are for those farther away.

An alternative to *a* is a number, either specific (*six, five, a thousand*) or general (*many, some, several, a few*). Like *a*, we do not continue using numbers by themselves after the first occurrence:

6.45a   He handed me six oranges and some cucumbers.

        *Six oranges were sour, but some cucumbers were good.

   b   He handed me six oranges and some cucumbers.
           The oranges were sour, but the cucumbers were good.
   c   He handed me six oranges and some cucumbers.
           The six oranges were sour, but the cucumbers were good.

If we want to continue using the number, we must also use *the* or one of the demonstratives. We have this same option with the indefinite article *a,* but we must make a change:

6.46a   In the refrigerator were an orange, an apple, and three bananas. *We shared an orange.
   b   In the refrigerator were an orange, an apple, and three bananas. We shared the orange.
   c   In the refrigerator were an orange, an apple, and three bananas. We shared the one orange.

Here we are not permitted to continue using *an,* but we may convert it to the etymologically related *one* and add *the.*

POSSESSIVES

In addition to articles and demonstratives, possessives are used to make common nouns refer to specific members of their class:

6.47   *Harold's* horse is getting too fat.
6.48   We mailed *Abner's* grandmother some persimmons.
6.49   That is *the cat's* bowl.
6.50   The court has appointed us *your* guardian.
6.51   The dog chased *its* tail.

In each example the possessive not only identifies the noun it modifies, but it also gives additional information in the way that demonstratives both identify and point out. This other information may be ownership:

6.52   *The woman's* purse was stolen.
6.53   Do you like *my* car?

At other times possession refers to parts of the body or qualities that we do not "own":

6.54   The man raised *his* arm.
6.55   *Marie's* intelligence is astounding.

Other possessives indicate the origin of the noun:

6.56   *The sun's* rays are bright.

Still others have a relationship with nouns similar to that of subject and verb or verb and object:

> **6.57** *Their* hatred for each other was horrifying. (Cf. They hated each other.)
>
> **6.58** She barely escaped from *her* pursuers. (Cf. People pursued her.)

And there are a variety of other relationships between the possessive and the noun it modifies: *a day's work* (measure), *actors' directions* (directions for actors), and the like. A sentence like the following can have several meanings:

> **6.59** Have you seen *my* painting?

Does *my painting* mean one that I own, one that I made, or one that was made of me? Since ownership is only one of many relationships between possessives and the nouns they modify, the word *possessive* may not be the best one. Other terms, such as *genitive,* are equally unsatisfactory, and no one has suggested anything better. Because of its widespread use, we shall continue to use *possessive,* noting its deficiencies.

In some ways possessives are like articles and demonstratives. As we have already noticed, all three can be used to designate a particular item. They are also mutually exclusive because a noun may be modified by only one of these words. We cannot, for example, combine an article and a demonstrative (*the those cookies, *that the ruby), an article and a possessive (*the Bill's house, *Bill's the house), or a demonstrative and a possessive (*this his rug, *her those socks). It may appear that a combination such as *this boy's dog* is an exception to the preceding observation, but we can readily show that *this* relates to *boy's,* not *dog.* We are pointing out the boy, not the dog. Also, if we change the number of either noun, *this* changes to *these* only if *boy's* is affected: *this boy's dogs, these boys' dogs, these boys' dog.* Another similarity among possessives, articles, and demonstratives is that singular nouns that can be counted must be preceded by one of these modifiers:

> **6.60a** *Car* is in *garage.*

We can say "one car, two cars, three cars" and "one garage, two garages, three garages." Nouns that name masses (*air, water, oil*) and a few others (*furniture*) are not counted, and they can be used without modifiers (*He tried to mix oil and water together*). Those that can be counted must be modified when they are singular, as we can see from **6.60a.** An adjective alone is not sufficient for making the sentence acceptable:

6.60b *Green car is in big garage.

However, an article, a demonstrative, or a possessive does make the sentence complete:

6.60c *The* car is in *that* garage.

d *My* car is in *your* garage.

Possessives are in many ways like articles and demonstratives.

But there are differences as well. The article *the* has the meaning "specific" and little else. The demonstratives include the meaning "specific" and also the notions of nearness and number (singular or plural). The possessives, by contrast, contain in addition to the notion of "specific" the full meaning of a noun or pronoun. In the following sentences we can illustrate these differences in meaning:

6.61a *The* coat fell to the floor.

b *That* coat fell to the floor.

c *Cynthia's* coat fell to the floor.

Possessives have more meaning than articles and demonstratives.

Also, possessives are noun phrases in themselves, whereas articles and demonstratives only modify nouns; that is, like other nouns, possessives are singular or plural:

6.62a He found *the woman's* money. (singular)

b He found *the women's* money. (plural)

Possessives may be modified by articles, demonstratives, other possessives, and adjectives:

6.63a He thanked *the children's* grandmother. (modified by the article *the*)

b He thanked *those children's* grandmother. (modified by the demonstrative *those*)

c He thanked *our children's* grandmother. (modified by the possessive *our*)

d He thanked *the unruly children's* grandmother. (modified by the adjective *unruly* and the article *the*)

Possessives can be modified by most of the structures that go with other nouns.

As noun phrases, possessives may be replaced with pronouns:

6.64a *The tall boy's* glasses are broken.

b *His* glasses are broken.

6.65a We were grading *those students'* papers.

b We were grading *their* papers.

We readily recognize *his* as meaning *the tall boy's* and *their* as referring to *those students'*.

Finally, possessives can usually be paraphrased with prepositional phrases:

6.66a   This is *my aunt's* friend.

  b   This is a friend *of my aunt*.

6.67a   *The book's* cover is torn.

  b   The cover *of the book* is torn.

Articles and demonstratives cannot be paraphrased in this way.

Possessives that precede the nouns they modify (e.g., *the book's, my*) are often called *inflected possessives;* those that appear in prepositional phrases are called *periphrastic possessives.* We usually use the inflected possessive for people and the periphrastic construction for nonhumans:

6.68   *Helen's* new job is exciting.

6.69   We need to replace the roof *of the barn*.

For this reason, we find the following sentence peculiar:

6.70a   The man who lives in the town's middle wrote something unkind on the page's bottom about the waist of Lucy.

We expect the possessives to be stated like this:

6.70b   The man who lives in the middle of town wrote something unkind on the bottom of the page about Lucy's waist.

That is, we do not expect the inflected possessive with the nonhuman nouns *middle* and *bottom,* but we do with the human noun *Lucy.*

However, there are other instances in which good writers depart from this customary practice. For example, we can find any of these:

6.71a   This is Nancy's picture.

  b   This is a picture of Nancy.

  c   This is a picture of Nancy's.

The **a** version is ambiguous, but **b** is not. The **c** version has only two meanings, as opposed to the three of **a**. Note that **c** has the inflected and the periphrastic formations combined. Other departures from the practice of using the inflected possessive for humans and the periphrastic for nonhumans can be seen in such structures as *the sun's rays, the dog's howl,* and *the car's tires.*

We usually find the periphrastic construction when the possessive noun phrase is long. We may feel comfortable with fairly short phrases such as **6.72a** and **6.73a,** but for longer ones we prefer the *of* phrase even for humans:

6.72a   *The man on the street's* opinion is often odd.

   b   The opinion *of the man on the street* is often odd.

6.73a   *The people next door's* dog kept me awake all night.

   b   The dog *of the people next door* kept me awake all night.

6.74a   *The people who live next door to my sister's* junk-filled yard is an eyesore.

   b   The junk-filled yard *of the people who live next door to my sister* is an eyesore.

Sentence **6.74a** illustrates one reason for preferring the periphrastic construction for long modifiers. Does the junk-filled yard belong to the people next door or to my sister? If the people live next door to my sister's junk-filled yard, we are saying, "The people is an eyesore," clearly an odd statement. A popular sentence of earlier grammarians was the following:

6.75   The daughter of Pharaoh's son is the son of Pharaoh's daughter.

At first reading, the meaning appears to be impossible. It is only when we realize that the possessive may relate to an entire phrase (*the daughter of Pharaoh*) as well as to a single word (*Pharaoh*) that the sentence makes sense.

Another potentially cumbersome structure is the sequence of possessives. There is usually no problem with one possessive modified by just one other:

6.76   *Maureen's husband's* cousin is a book salesman.

6.77   I accepted *my nephew's* suggestion.

6.78   *My wife's* grandfather was there.

But if we have more than two possessives in succession, the meaning becomes confusing:

6.79   My wife's first husband's only child's grandfather was there.

We could have extended the structure even further by letting it be the grandfather's nurse who was there, but the sentence is sufficiently confusing as it is.

Since many people hesitate over the written representation of inflected possessives, let us look at the rules for their formation:

1. For singular nouns, add an apostrophe and *s*: *girl* (singular), *girl's* (possessive); *Danny, Danny's*.
2. For plural nouns ending in *s*, add an apostrophe: *boys* (plural), *boys'* (possessive); *dentists, dentists'*.
3. For plural nouns not ending in *s*, add an apostrophe and *s*: *women* (plural), *women's* (possessive); *firemen, firemen's*.
4. Proper nouns not ending in *s* in the singular follow the same rules as common nouns: *Bob, Bob's* (singular); *Bobs, Bobs'* (plural).
5. Proper nouns ending in *s* in the singular may follow the same rules as other proper nouns: *Mr. Jones, Mr. Jones's* (singular); *the Joneses, the Joneses'* (plural). However, there is an option in that the singular possessive may be *Mr. Jones'*, the form that is normally used by people who pronounce it as one syllable.
6. Indefinite pronouns follow the same rules as nouns: *someone's, nobody's, something's, everyone's, no one's*.
7. Personal pronouns do not have an apostrophe: *yours, hers, his, ours, theirs, its*. The possessive *its* is distinguished from the contraction of *it is*, which is written *it's*.

ADJECTIVES

Instead of limiting a class by the use of an article, a demonstrative, or a possessive, we may use adjectives such as *loud, horrible, green,* or *slovenly*. For example, if we want to divide towns into subclasses, we have several means available: *small towns* or *large towns, ugly towns* or *pretty towns, backward towns* or *progressive towns*. In each subdivision we have somewhat arbitrarily created a dichotomy so that a town that does not belong in one category (e.g., *ugly*) belongs in the other (*pretty*). The criteria for placing a town in one category or the other may be entirely subjective, or they may be objective as in the case of size.

As we are making subdivisions of a set of objects, we are not limited to two categories. For example, we may have three divisions: *small, medium-sized,* and *large*. Or there may be four: *northern, eastern, southern,* and *western*. Depending upon our interests, we may segment the class however we choose. If our interests lie in nationalities, we may divide towns into *Mexican towns, Bulgarian towns, Chinese towns,* and so on, until we run out of countries. For other objects, we may make subdivisions according to colors, breaking the color spectrum at as many or as few places as we choose.

We can see the limiting function of adjectives in the following sentences:

6.80a   My sister bought *a dog*.

    b   My sister bought *a huge dog.*

6.81a Harold has become *an editor.*

    b   Harold has become *an excellent editor.*

6.82a I consider him *a prude.*

    b   I consider him *a silly prude.*

6.83a We are buying *a car.*

    b   We are buying *a new car.*

In each of these sentences the adjective serves to limit the noun to a subclass of the set; in none of them does it make the noun one specific entity.

Often we use adjectives for their own sake, in which case they may be more important than the nouns they modify:

6.84a I have *an arm.*

    b   I have *a sore arm.*

6.85a That certainly is *a sunset.*

    b   That certainly is *a beautiful sunset.*

In these sentences the **a** versions are uninteresting because they give information that the listener or reader presumably knows. Although the adjectives in the **b** versions do serve to limit the class (sore vs. healthy arms, beautiful vs. unspectacular sunsets), our purpose is to comment on soreness or beauty, not to limit the nouns. It should not be assumed that the only reason we use adjectives is to restrict subclasses of nouns.

In addition to using different adjectives that contrast, such as *tall* and *short,* we sometimes speak of greater or lesser degrees: *tall, taller, tallest; delightful, more delightful, most delightful; friendly, less friendly, the least friendly.* Thus, if we consider two ropes to be short, we do not distinguish them if we say, "Bring me the short rope." We can say, "Bring me the *shorter* rope." Most adjectives of one syllable and some of two syllables take comparatives in *-er* and superlatives in *-est.* A number of adjectives with two syllables and most that are longer form comparisons with *more* and *most* or *less* and *least.*

At times we do not content ourselves with a single adjective to modify a noun but use two or more:

    6.86 I had to read a *long, dull, complicated* article.

    6.87 Those *tall, stately* trees are beautiful.

Whenever two or more adjectives can be interchanged (*dull, long, complicated* in **6.86**) or permit the placement of *and* between them (*tall and stately* in **6.87**), they are said to be **coordinate,** and we separate them with commas. Since articles, demonstratives, numbers, possessives, and adjectives are different kinds of modifiers, they do not permit rearrangement or the insertion of *and;* we, therefore, do not place commas between these types of modifiers, such as between *a* and *long* in **6.86** or between *those* and *tall* in **6.87.** In **6.88,** we see another kind of modifier that does not form a coordinate sequence:

> **6.88**   He built a tall stone fence.

Because *stone* names the material of which the fence is made, it is different from *tall;* hence, there is no comma separating *tall* and *stone.* We could not say "a stone tall fence" or "a tall and stone fence."

Although adjectives are like articles, demonstratives, and possessives in that they may limit nouns, they are different from these other words:

1. Whereas adjectives may show comparison, the others do not (*happy, happier; *this, thiser*).
2. Although there may be several adjectives preceding a noun (*an old, helpless, gray dog*), not more than one member of the other classes may occur there (**my your books*).
3. If a noun has an article, a demonstrative, or a possessive, the other two are prohibited. It is possible, however, to have one of these words and a following adjective (**the that rug; the new rug*).
4. When a noun has an article, a demonstrative, or a possessive as well as an adjective before it, the adjective follows the other word (*a blue flower, *blue a flower; that naughty girl, *naughty that girl*).
5. An adjective has more semantic content than an article or a demonstrative, and it restricts the noun to a subclass, not to a unique member.
6. A singular count noun must have an article, a demonstrative, or a possessive accompanying it (*The glass broke. *Glass broke*). An adjective will not fulfill this requirement (**Pretty glass broke*).

Some books refer to articles, demonstratives, possessives, and numbers as **determiners** to distinguish them from adjectives.

COMPOUNDS

The adjective plus noun construction looks very much like another with a slightly different meaning, the **compound:**

Compound	*Modifier + Noun*
a blackboard	a black board
a sick room	a sick child
a redhead	a red head
a dumbwaiter	a dumb waiter
a cannon ball	a large ball

We do not think of a *blackboard* as just any board that is black, nor is a *sick room* a room that is sick, although a *sick child* is a child that is sick. We recognize differences between the other pairs. Each of the modifier-plus-noun combinations can be paraphrased with "A _____ that is _____" as "A waiter that is dumb." The compounds do not permit this paraphrase. In addition, the modifier-plus-noun combinations can be altered by changing the adjective: *a black board, a green board, a yellow board;* the compounds do not permit such substitution. We also notice a difference in pronunciation. The heavier stress is on the second element, the noun, in the modifier-plus-noun constructions; in the compounds it is on the first element.

Let us look at a typical contrast:

6.89 We ate *a hot dog.*

6.90 We chased *a hot dog.*

In **6.89,** we are speaking of a wiener on a bun, and we would be upset if someone served us a hot dog made with dog meat. In **6.90,** we mean a canine that is hot. This difference in meaning is matched by the one in pronunciation that we mentioned in the last paragraph. For the food, we stress *hot* more than we do *dog;* for the animal we place heavier stress on *dog.*

Sometimes compounds are spelled as separate words, as we can see with *a hot dog, a sick room,* and *a cannon ball.* Others are spelled without a space between their components: *hotbed, scarecrow, leap-frog, roommate, snapshot, housekeeper.* Still others are hyphenated: *mother-in-law, water-repellent, high-octane.* The usual progression is for a compound to start out spelled as two separate words (*basket ball*). It is later hyphenated (*basket-ball*), and finally it is written solid (*basketball*).

The meaning of a compound is often more restricted than that of an adjective plus noun. For example, *a black bird,* adjective plus noun meaning "bird that is black," restricts the class of birds to those of a single color, including crows, buzzards, and others. The compound *blackbird,* however, is a further restriction to one group of birds that are black. Similarly, a *sidewalk* is not just any walkway that goes to the side.

With *sidewalk* we see another feature of compounds. We tend to think of them as single units, not as two separate words, and we often lose track of their original meaning. For many sidewalks, the first component is not very meaningful; we, therefore, see nothing strange about a sidewalk that is placed in the middle of a yard. Similarly, we find nothing incongruous with eating *a cold hot dog,* taking an examination in *a pink bluebook,* or writing on *a green blackboard.*

Since compounds function as single words, we shall consider them as units, regardless of how they are spelled. The noun phrase *a small high chair* will, therefore, be said to consist of an article (*a*), an adjective (*small*), and a noun (*high chair*).

The semantic relationship between the parts of a compound can be any of several possibilities. *A bird dog* is a dog that hunts birds, but *bird seed* is a seed that birds eat. A *bird bath* is a bath for birds, and a *bird brain* is a person with a brain like that of a bird. A *bird lover* is a person who loves birds, unless we are reading imaginative literature, in which case it may be a bird that is in love. Turning to other words, a *redhead* and a *blackhead* normally have nothing in common. Compounds with *horse* as the first element show an especially wide range of meanings: *horse show, horse laugh, horse doctor, horse tail, horse feed, horse breeder, horse race, horse fly, horse disease, horse opera,* and others. Many compounds with animal names as the first element show metaphoric comparisons: *an eagle eye, a cat nap, a rat nest, rabbit ears, a cow lick, horse feathers, a wolf whistle, a sheepskin, a pigskin, a bear hug, the fox trot.*

It is possible to expand compounds. For example, by combining *base* and *ball* we obtain *baseball.* If we add this to *club*, we get *baseball club.* A baseball club composed of amateurs is an *amateur baseball club.* If this club is in a small town, it is a *small-town amateur baseball club.* Other extended compounds include *a fifty-mile radius, volunteer fire department, weekend house guest, double-barreled shotgun auction,* and the like. The fact that many of these are spelled as separate words makes them less obvious than they would be if we spelled them solid: *weekendhouseguest.* Even a cursory inspection of a daily newspaper or a current magazine will show many examples. As we said earlier, they function as single units and are not treated as modifier plus noun constructions.

EXERCISES

A. Replace each noun phrase in the following sentences with a pronoun:

1. Those three wooly coats are Robert's.
2. My generous aunt has given my money to that beggar.
3. Where did the gray mother cat find her young kitten?
4. Does your nephew like this dreadful city?
5. That last ham sandwich tasted peculiar.

B. Replace the proper nouns with common nouns that refer to the same people or objects. You may use articles and possessives but no other modifiers. How is meaning affected with your substitutions?

1. Brenda Farrell sailed on the *Queen Elizabeth* yesterday.
2. In January we made an exciting trip to the Himalayas.
3. The Statue of Liberty was a gift from France.
4. When I read *The Heart of Midlothian* this time, Jeannie Deans seemed more stupid than ever.
5. He will be staying at the St. Francis while he is in San Francisco.
6. Mr. Pruitt assured Paul that the Xerox Corporation would be happy to send him the information he requested.
7. Mother took a cab to Kennedy Airport.
8. Does the Mississippi River flow through Louisiana?
9. Do you like your new Mercury?
10. He thought he saw the President crossing Pennsylvania Avenue.

C. Replace the common nouns with proper nouns:

1. That planet is closer to our planet than this one is.
2. Did the woman travel far up the river?
3. One day last month my friend bought a car.
4. I rode to a city on a train.
5. That man has been talking to the devil.
6. In the forest the outlaw has made his home.
7. Was that man living in this county then?
8. I flew from one continent to another continent in two hours.
9. Is the bank open on this holiday?
10. I was eating in a restaurant.

D. Use a definite article, a demonstrative, or a possessive to make each of the nouns in the following sentences more specific:

1. A man was whistling a tune.
2. A dog ran under a car.
3. An uncle handed an attendant a key.
4. Would you like pickles on a sandwich?
5. A nurse became a friend.

E. Write the possessives of the following nouns and pronouns:

1. bird	6. no one
2. birds	7. ox
3. someone	8. Ray Pearce
4. he	9. sheep
5. Louise Percy	10. it

11. man   16. the Smiths
12. men   17. Dr. Adams
13. they   18. Charles
14. grandfather   19. you
15. Senator Sanders   20. who

F. Make the nouns in the following sentences more specific by adding adjectives. Some of your adjectives may be commonplace (*little, old, brown,* etc.), but the others should be more imaginative.

1. The woman suddenly skated to the window.
2. His teacher lives in that apartment.
3. This chair belongs in the room.
4. Some children were giggling hysterically at your shoes.
5. The speech did not interest the people.
6. That hotel looked welcome to the traveler.
7. This snow is upsetting your babysitter.
8. Where can a shopper find a carton of eggs in this store?
9. The witch hovered in the air.
10. The woman dropped crumbs on the floor.

G. On a sheet of paper draw three columns labeled *Noun, Adjective,* and *Adverb.* Place each of the words given below under the appropriate column, and add or remove suffixes to provide the other two forms. That is, if *stupid* were given, you would write it under the adjective column and then provide the adverb *stupidly* and the noun *stupidity.* If you were given *wretchedly,* you would write it under the adverb column and provide the noun *wretchedness* and the adjective *wretched.*

1. duty   6. beautiful
2. accurately   7. fatally
3. carefully   8. nervous
4. kindness   9. cruelty
5. zeal   10. rigidly

H. Write compounds using the following words as the last element. For some of them, use expanded compounds such as *week-end house guest.*

1. door   6. paper
2. window   7. party
3. man   8. school
4. truck   9. dress
5. pen   10. club

I. The combination of certain adjectives and nouns is odd or, at times, nonsensical: *a brown curiosity, a groovy whippersnapper, a chic chick, a gossipy madonna,* and the like. Explain why these examples are odd. Saying that curiosity cannot be brown is true, but it does not explain why the noun phrase will be equally odd if we substitute *blue, purple, aqua,* or any other color. After you have explained these four examples, add ten others and explain why the adjectives are inappropriate for the given nouns.

J. Poets sometimes use unconventional adjective-noun combinations for special reasons, such as Blake's "youthful Harlot's curse" or Hopkins' "dapple-dawn-drawn Falcon." Find three or four examples of such unusual combinations in poetry and explain what the poet is trying to do with them. Note: Merely saying that the poet does it "for effect" is not satisfactory. Explain what effect is created.

7

Clauses and Phrases that Modify Nouns

In the last chapter we saw that there are several ways to designate which member of a class we are indicating. One of these is to use the definite article *the,* which shows that the object has been previously identified, either in a previous statement or from shared knowledge:

> **7.1** At the zoo we saw an orangutan and a baboon. *The* orangutan interested me more than *the* baboon did.
>
> **7.2** *The* Principal will talk with you now.

Another way of specifying individuals is by pointing them out with demonstratives:

> **7.3** *These* cookies are too sweet.
>
> **7.4** Who is *that* pest?

Possessives provide a third means:

> **7.5** *Our* clock must be fast.
>
> **7.6** Have you ridden in *Dick's* car?

Or we can use adjectives:

> **7.7** The teacher likes *inquisitive* children.
>
> **7.8** He went to the *new* courthouse.

In each of these sentences we are indicating either a specific member of the class (*that pest, Dick's car, the new courthouse*) or a subclass (*inquisitive children*).

In many sentences the modifier carries a meaning at least as important as that of the noun:

> **7.9a** He brought me some cherries.
>
> **b** He brought me some ripe cherries.
>
> **7.10a** Do you like poems?
>
> **b** Do you like my poems?
>
> **7.11a** We gave her some water.
>
> **b** We gave her some poisoned water.

But even for sentences such as these, the modifier still limits.

RELATIVE CLAUSES

Instead of defining an object by pointing it out, naming its characteristics, and the like, we often relate it to a specific event or state. For example, we may start with this sentence:

> **7.12** Lorraine was hit by *a car*.

If we want to indicate which car hit her, we may do so with the devices we have already considered (*that car, your car, an old car*). Or we may say something else about it:

> **7.13** The car was driven by a maniac.
>
> **7.14** The car was barely moving.

We can combine either sentence **7.13** or **7.14** with **7.12** and obtain the following:

> **7.15** Lorraine was hit by a car *that was driven by a maniac.*
>
> **7.16** Lorraine was hit by a car *that was barely moving.*

In each of these sentences we are limiting the class of cars by means of a structure that is known as a **relative clause.**

Relative clauses can be paraphrased with complete sentences, such as **7.13** and **7.14,** which contain an instance of the same noun as that modified (i.e., *car*). Here are some other examples:

7.17a   The bottle was empty. The bottle rolled down the aisle.

   b   The bottle *that rolled down the aisle* was empty.

7.18a   The man was angry. The man hit me.

   b   The man *who hit me* was angry.

In each case we decide which act or state is to be used for purposes of identification. In **7.17b,** we are stating that the bottle was empty and using the relative clause to tell the reader which bottle is meant. In **7.18b,** *who hit me* tells which man was angry. If the writer had had a different meaning in mind, the following sentences might have resulted:

7.17c   The bottle *that was empty* rolled down the aisle.

7.18c   The man *who was angry* hit me.

Now we are using the relative clauses to tell the reader which bottle rolled down the aisle and which man hit me. From pairs of sentences in isolation, such as **7.17a** and **7.18a,** there is usually no way to tell which is the more important and which is to serve an identifying function. If the sentences occur in a larger context and if we know the intent of the speaker or writer, however, there is only one choice. We say that the sentence which serves an identifying function is **subordinated** to the other one.

Relative clauses are generally introduced by the **relative pronouns** *who, whom, that, which,* and *whose:*

7.19   She reprimanded the waiter [*who* spilled the soup].

7.20   Judy Reynolds is a woman [*whom* we respect greatly].

7.21   The car [*that* I bought] is almost new.

7.22   The movie [*which* you saw] was a rerun.

7.23   I saw the man [*whose* house was burglarized].

Like interrogative pronouns, relatives occur at the beginning of the sentence to which they belong, and they may stand for any noun phrase, whether it is a subject, a direct object, an object of a preposition, or any other function:

7.24a   *The glass* broke. (subject)

   b   *that* broke

   c   The glass [that broke] belonged to my grandmother.

7.25a   We bought *the milk.* (direct object)

   b   *that* we bought

   c   The milk [that we bought] tasted peculiar.

7.26a She showed *the man* the letter. (indirect object)

    b *whom* she showed the letter

    c The man [whom she showed the letter] stole it.

7.27a You are referring to *the short story*. (object of a preposition)

    b to *which* you are referring

    c The short story [to which you are referring] was written by Faulkner.

7.28a They called him *a name*. (objective complement)

    b *that* they called him

    c The name [that they called him] was degrading.

In each sentence the relative pronoun occurs at the beginning of the clause and not at the usual place for a direct object, an objective complement, or the like.

Although relative pronouns may look somewhat like interrogatives, this similarity is largely confined to their being positioned at the beginning. For the interrogatives, we do not know what is being referred to, but for the relatives we do know the referent. Furthermore, interrogative pronouns introduce questions, but relative pronouns do not. Instead of eliciting information, relative pronouns introduce clauses that modify nouns.

Who and *whom* are used to refer only to humans, *which* to nonhumans, and *that* to either.

7.29a I picked up the boy [*who* fell from the roof].

    b *I picked up the boy [*which* fell from the roof].

    c I picked up the boy [*that* fell from the roof].

7.30a *I picked up the rock [*who* fell from the roof].

    b I picked up the rock [*which* fell from the roof].

    c I picked up the rock [*that* fell from the roof].

Many people feel more comfortable using *whose* to refer to humans than to nonhumans:

7.31 I hit the man [*whose* language disgusted me].

7.32 ?I sold the chair [*whose* color disgusted me].

However, there is no satisfactory substitute for nonhumans, and a structure such as the following is awkward:

7.33 I sold the chair [the color of which disgusted me].

To avoid sentences like **7.33,** many people accept the use of *whose* for nonhumans.

When the relative pronoun is the object of a preposition, the preposition may be found either at the beginning of the clause or at the end:

>**7.34a**   The people [*about* whom we were talking] left.
>
>   **b**   The people [whom we were talking *about*] left.

The **b** version with the preposition at the end of the clause is less formal than the **a** version. For such sentences some people prefer to use the informal *who* to maintain a consistent style:

>**7.34c**   The people [who we were talking about] left.

With objects of prepositions there are restrictions on the use of the pronoun *that:*

>**7.34d**   The people [*that* we were talking about] left.
>
>   **e**   *The people [about *that* we were talking] left.

Whereas *that* is possible when the preposition comes at the end of the clause, it is not allowed when the preposition precedes it.

At times the relative pronoun is understood but does not actually occur:

>**7.35a**   The picture [that you drew] wasn't very good.
>
>   **b**   The picture [you drew] wasn't very good.
>
>**7.36a**   The people [whom we showed the letter] laughed.
>
>   **b**   The people [we showed the letter] laughed.
>
>**7.37a**   I met the woman [whom you were pointing to].
>
>   **b**   I met the woman [you were pointing to].

Yet there are restrictions:

>**7.37c**   *I met the woman [to you were pointing].
>
>   **d**   I met the woman [to whom you were pointing].

When a preposition precedes a relative pronoun, it may not be omitted. Also relative pronouns functioning as subjects must be present:

>**7.38a**   I despise people [who laugh at me].
>
>   **b**   *I despise people [laugh at me].

Only object pronouns may be omitted — direct objects, indirect objects, objective complements, and objects of prepositions. Relative pronouns that are objects of prepositions may be omitted only if the prepositions do not precede them.

When a noun is modified by a relative clause and adjectives, it may become quite long:

> **7.39** *The old woman who lives across the street* found the coin.

The italicized structure consists of a noun (*woman*) that is modified by an article (*the*), an adjective (*old*), and a relative clause (*who lives across the street*). The entire structure is a noun phrase, just as *the woman* is, even though other structures are contained within it. We can readily show that the entire structure is a noun phrase by having a pronoun replace it:

> **7.40** *She* found the coin.
>
> **7.41** *Who* found the coin?

Also, if we turn the sentence into a passive, it is the entire structure that follows *by:*

> **7.42** The coin was found by *the old woman who lives across the street.*

As we continue to expand noun phrases by adding modifiers, many of them will become even longer than this one; however, if we are able to analyze them and remember that they function just as single words do, they will present no problems.

PARTICIPIAL PHRASES

For economy we often reduce relative clauses to more compact structures known as *participial phrases;* that is, instead of using full relative clauses like the **a** versions below, we use the **b** versions:

> **7.43a** The snow [that is falling today] isn't sticking.
>
> **b** The snow [falling today] isn't sticking.
>
> **7.44a** I startled the man [who is sitting by the window].
>
> **b** I startled the man [sitting by the window].
>
> **7.45a** We ran to the girl [who was motioning to us].
>
> **b** We ran to the girl [motioning to us].

Participial phrases can be paraphrased with relative clauses that contain a form of *be.* They do not contain relative pronouns, nor do they show tense.

We can illustrate the absence of tense with the following sentences:

7.46a   The salesman [who was knocking at the door] irritated me.

   b   The salesman [knocking at the door] irritated me.

7.47a   The salesman [who is knocking at the door] irritated me.

   b   The salesman [knocking at the door] irritated me.

The acts of knocking and irritating may or may not have occurred at the same time, and they are not necessarily related. Whether the knocking occurred prior to the act of speaking or simultaneously with it, it still appears as *knocking at the door*. This distinction is found in the full clause in the tense of *be: was* or *is*. There is no such indication for the participle.

Participles ending in -*ing* are traditionally known as *present participles,* as opposed to *past participles* such as those in the **b** sentences below:

7.48a   The woman [who was pushed down the stairs] was not hurt.

   b   The woman [pushed down the stairs] was not hurt.

7.49a   We pitied the man [who was mauled by the lion].

   b   We pitied the man [mauled by the lion].

7.50a   The letter [that was written by Carolyn] was funny.

   b   The letter [written by Carolyn] was funny.

As comparison of the **a** and **b** versions shows, past participial phrases can be paraphrased with passive relative clauses containing *be*. As the name suggests, past participial phrases begin with past participles, the same form that follows the auxiliary *have* and the passive *be:*

7.51   We have *chosen* the winner.

7.52   The winner was *chosen* by us.

7.53   The man *chosen* by us will not fail.

Like present participial phrases, they do not show tense:

7.54a   The people [who are insulted by your remarks] will be unfriendly.

   b   The people [insulted by your remarks] will be unfriendly.

7.55a   The people [who were insulted by your remarks] will be unfriendly.

   b   The people [insulted by your remarks] will be unfriendly.

Whereas relative clauses change for tense, participial phrases do not.

The terms *present participle* and *past participle* are unfortunate because they suggest present and past tense. Both participles may denote action taking place at the same time as another act in the sentence or as the time of the utterance. More accurate names would be *active* and *passive participles* because they correspond to active and passive relative clauses, respectively. A few examples will illustrate:

7.56a   The man [who is kicking the horse] will suffer.

    b   The man [kicking the horse] will suffer.

    c   The man [who was kicked by the horse] will suffer.

    d   The man [kicked by the horse] will suffer.

7.57a   The postman [who was biting the dog] will get rabies.

    b   The postman [biting the dog] will get rabies.

    c   The postman [who is bitten by the dog] will get rabies.

    d   The postman [bitten by the dog] will get rabies.

The **a** and **b** sentences identify the man or postman by an action that he performed; in the **c** and **d** sentences the action happened to him. The two kinds of participles show active and passive voice, not present and past time. In spite of these problems, the names *present* and *past participle* are so widely used that we will continue to use them, noting that they do not refer to tense.

Although participles do not express tense, they do tell whether the action is in progress or completed. The present participle is always progressive, as we see when we paraphrase it with a verb in a relative clause:

7.58a   The burglar [who is robbing your house] will be disappointed.

    b   The burglar [robbing your house] will be disappointed.

Sentences **7.58a** and **7.58b** both contain active phrases or clauses. There is also a passive progressive. Like any other passive, it is formed with the auxiliary *be* followed by the past participle:

7.59a   The house [that is being robbed by a burglar] belongs to the Lambs.

    b   The house [being robbed by a burglar] belongs to the Lambs.

In addition, there are perfect participles, formed with the auxiliary *have;* as we saw in Chapter 3, the auxiliary *have* is followed by a past participle:

7.60a   My sister, [who has bought a new car], is now impecuni-
ous.

   b   My sister, [having bought a new car], is now impecuni-
ous.

And there is a perfect passive participle:

7.61a   The woman [who had been invited to the reception]
laughed with embarrassment.

   b   The woman, [having been invited to the reception],
laughed with embarrassment.

In the preceding sentence, we see the auxiliary *have* followed by the
past participle *been* and the passive *be* followed by the past participle
invited. Theoretically it is possible to have a final combination of auxiliaries with a participle, *have,* and the progressive *be:*

7.62a   Those people [who have been sneering at me all night]
finally left.

   b   Those people, [having been sneering at me all night],
finally left.

As the forced nature of this example shows, this structure is rarely
found.

Like verbs, participles may take complements and adverbial
modifiers:

Direct Object

7.63a   The person [who is hitting *me*] had better stop.

   b   The person [hitting *me*] had better stop.

Predicate Adjective

7.64a   The girl [who was looking *unhappy*] left the room.

   b   The girl [looking *unhappy*] left the room.

Objective Complement

7.65a   Anyone [who is calling me *stupid*] will get hit.

   b   Anyone [calling me *stupid*] will get hit.

7.66a The people [who were talking *in the hallway*] disturbed me.

b The people [talking *in the hallway*] disturbed me.

Furthermore, as we saw with past participles, they may be passive. These similarities between participles and verbs are not surprising if we think of participial phrases as reduced relative clauses. With such an interpretation, they *are* verbs that have had tense removed. Also, it is not the participle alone that modifies a noun but the entire participial phrase, just as it is the entire relative clause that modifies, not just the verb in it.

When a participle is intransitive and has no modifiers, it often occurs before the noun, the same as an adjective:

7.67a A dog [that is snarling] is dangerous.

b A [snarling] dog is dangerous.

7.68a We hid the letter [that was opened].

b We hid the [opened] letter.

Unlike adjectives, some participles may follow the noun:

7.69a A *smiling* beggar is suspicious.

b A beggar *smiling* is suspicious.

7.70a A *richly dressed* beggar is suspicious.

b A beggar *richly dressed* is suspicious.

7.71a A *handsome* beggar is suspicious.

b *A beggar *handsome* is suspicious.

Whereas **7.71b** might be acceptable in poetry, it is impossible in prose.

ADVERBIALS

It is traditionally assumed that only adjectives can modify nouns, but adverbials of place often do so as well. For example, we can readily find examples like the **b** versions below:

7.72a The people [who are outside] are noisy.

b The people [outside] are noisy.

7.73a   The books [that are there] are valuable.

   b   The books [there] are valuable.

7.74a   I was talking to the man [who was ahead].

   b   I was talking to the man [ahead].

Prepositional phrases may also modify nouns:

7.75a   The coat [that is on the chair] is wet.

   b   The coat [on the chair] is wet.

7.76a   The people [who were between the cars] frightened me.

   b   The people [between the cars] frightened me.

Note that these structures are clearly adverbials of place when the full relative clause is given, as in the **a** versions. If we consider the **b** versions as reduced relative clauses, it no longer seems strange that adverbials of place appear to modify nouns.

RESTRICTIVE AND NONRESTRICTIVE MODIFIERS

The noun modifiers that we have examined so far serve the function of restricting the class of objects under discussion, either to a subclass or to a unique individual. In the following sentence, for example, the relative clause indicates which boy is intended:

7.77   I threw the sandwich to the boy [who stood behind Al].

Some nouns are shown to be unique by other means, such as the following:

7.78   I threw the sandwich to Raul, [who stood behind Al].

Here the proper noun identifies the person, and the relative clause gives added information. In fact, sentence **7.78** could almost be paraphrased with a compound sentence:

7.79   I threw the sandwich to Raul, and he stood behind Al.

A compound sentence such as this loses the notion of subordination found in **7.78**; it is, therefore, not a real paraphrase. We call a modifier that does not serve the function of restricting the class of objects named a *nonrestrictive modifier;* those that restrict are called *restrictive modifiers.*

Here are some additional examples of restrictive and nonrestrictive modifiers:

7.80a We discussed the movie [that we had seen four times].

b We discussed *Gone With the Wind*, [which we had seen four times].

7.81a The city [that I visited last week] has hot summers.

b Chicago, [which I visited last week], has hot summers.

7.82a She wrote a paper on the planet [that she had been observing through a telescope].

b She wrote a paper on Mars, [which she had been observing through a telescope].

7.83a The actress [whom I admire so much] is in a new play.

b Lucy Conlin, [whom I admire so much], is in a new play.

In the **b** sentences the proper noun is already identified; the nonrestrictive clause merely supplies added information. In the **a** versions, however, we do not know which movie, city, planet, or actress is intended without the restrictive clause.

At times there are several people or objects with the same name, making the noun common. In such instances the article *the* and a **restrictive clause are found:**

7.84 The Helen Adams [to whom I referred] is not associated with this firm.

7.85 Which of the Springfields [that are in the Midwest] do you mean?

7.86 *The Secret Agent* [that I recommended to you] is the one by Joseph Conrad.

In each of these sentences, the relative clause is restrictive.

At other times a possessive or adjective specifies the noun, and the relative clause is nonrestrictive. In the **a** versions below, the clause is restrictive; in the **b** versions, nonrestrictive:

7.87a I was talking to a mother [who detests poems about motherhood].

b I was talking to Sheila's mother, [who detests poems about motherhood].

7.88a Her daughter [who lives in Columbus] is an ornithologist.

b Her youngest daughter, [who lives in Columbus], is an ornithologist.

7.89a We were discussing his grandmother [who is skiing in the Alps].

    b We were discussing his maternal grandmother, [who is skiing in the Alps].

Once we label the noun as *Sheila's mother, her youngest daughter,* or *his maternal grandmother,* we know which one is meant.

    Shared knowledge may be enough to restrict a noun. For example, if the speaker can assume that the listener knows he has only one brother, he may say the following:

    7.90 My brother, [who went to Greece last summer], brought back some interesting post cards.

The designation *my brother* is enough to indicate which one is meant. Similarly, if we know that Bob has only one car, *Bob's car* is enough to specify the object we are discussing, and any accompanying relative clause will be nonrestrictive. If we are speaking of our solar system, *the sun* indicates the source of light that is meant; similarly, we may refer to *the moon* to indicate the heavenly body that circles the earth.

    When we examine relative clauses with indefinite pronouns or adjectives, we discover a peculiar relationship. Notice the difference in meaning between the **a** sentences with the restrictive clauses and the **b** sentences without them:

    7.91a Anyone [who remembers these directions] can find my house easily.

       b Anyone can find my house easily.

    7.92a All teachers [who turn their grades in on time] will be rewarded.

       b All teachers will be rewarded.

In sentences such as these, the clauses still function to limit the class (*ones, teachers*). In **7.92a**, for example, of all the teachers in existence, it is only those who turn their grades in on time who will be rewarded. However, the **b** sentences are not just less specific versions of the **a** sentences; they mean something different. The indefinite word — *any, all, each, every* — is closely tied to the relative clause, and if we omit one we must omit the other as well. Unfortunately, too much emphasis on sentences like **7.91** and **7.92** led some earlier grammarians to state that a restrictive clause is essential to the meaning of the sentence, whereas a nonrestrictive clause is not. Such a statement is absurd; unless the nonrestrictive modifier is redundant, it is as essential to "meaning" as the restrictive modifier is. The two differ in that one serves a limiting function and the other does not.

The semantic differences between restrictive and nonrestrictive clauses are matched with those of intonation and choice of relative pronoun. Nonrestrictive clauses are set off by pauses in speech and by commas in writing:

7.93a   The Dean, [who listens to all grade complaints], is out of town this week.

If the school has only one dean or if the context makes it clear which one is meant (e.g., the conversation takes place in a certain dean's office), the relative clause is nonrestrictive. On the other hand, if the clause is used to indicate a particular dean, it is restrictive:

7.93b   The dean [who listens to all grade complaints] is out of town this week.

Comma intonation is found with the nonrestrictive clause but not with the restrictive.

For restrictive clauses the full range of relative pronouns may be selected: *who, whom, which, whose, that*. For nonrestrictives, *that* is not permitted.

7.94a   She scolded the child [*that* was playing in the mud].

b   *She scolded Barry, [*that* was playing in the mud].

Nonrestrictive clauses permit only *who/whom* for humans, *which* for nonhumans, and *whose* for possessives.

Another difference between the two kinds of clauses can be seen in the deletability of the relative pronoun. Object relatives may be deleted in restrictive clauses, but they must be retained in nonrestrictives:

7.95a   The city [we visited last spring] was interesting.

b   *Atlanta, [we visited last spring], was interesting.

c   Atlanta, [which we visited last spring], was interesting.

Restrictive and nonrestrictive clauses differ not only in meaning, but also in form.

What we have said about clauses is also largely true of participial phrases:

7.96a   My brother [who was standing by the curb] was almost hit by a car.

b   My brother [standing by the curb] was almost hit by a car.

7.97a My youngest brother, [who was standing by the curb], was almost hit by a car.

b My youngest brother, [standing by the curb], was almost hit by a car.

In **7.96**, both the relative clause and the participial phrase identify which brother is meant, even though his position is unquestionably important. In **7.97**, however, the word *youngest* identifies the brother; the clause or phrase is important only for the information it contains, not for identifying the noun.

Unlike clauses, nonrestrictive participial phrases may occur at various places in the sentence, not just directly after the nouns they modify. For example, any of these versions is possible:

7.98a Brenda, [leaning out the window], called loudly.

b [Leaning out the window], Brenda called loudly.

c Brenda called loudly, [leaning out the window].

Such freedom does not exist with clauses:

7.99a Brenda, [who was leaning out the window], called loudly.

b *[Who was leaning out the window], Brenda called loudly.

c *Brenda called loudly, [who was leaning out the window].

In fact, the position of nonrestrictive participial phrases at the beginning or the end of the sentence is more usual for many writers than that directly after the noun.

We may paraphrase sentences with nonrestrictive participial phrases as compound sentences, as we did nonrestrictive clauses:

7.100a Laughing obstreperously, Harry declined the invitation.

b Harry was laughing obstreperously, and he declined the invitation.

They may also be paraphrased in most cases with adverbial clauses:

7.100c While he was laughing obstreperously, Harry declined the invitation.

Or with the following structure:

7.100d While laughing obstreperously, Harry declined the invitation.

Some grammarians call *while laughing obstreperously* an **elliptical clause** because it seems to have *he was* omitted. However, this is inconsistent unless we are prepared to call all participial phrases elliptical clauses, because they can all be looked upon as reduced relative clauses.

EXERCISES

A. Replace the complex noun phrases in the following sentences with proper nouns.

> **example:**   The man who opened the door insulted everyone.
> *Harry* insulted everyone.

1. Did you thank the taxi driver who found your gloves?
2. Someone sent my friend who lives in Tucson a magazine subscription.
3. I stayed for a month in that city on the Seine.
4. The man climbing that mountain will probably fall.
5. Did you see the movie that everyone is raving about?

B. Enclose each relative clause in brackets and draw an arrow to the noun it modifies. Then paraphrase the clause with a complete sentence and tell how the relative pronoun functions.

> **example:**   I finally killed the fly [that had been bothering me].
> Paraphrase: The fly had been bothering me.
> *That* functions as subject.

1. We found a door that was unlocked.
2. Her mother considers her a person whom everyone should admire.
3. We handed it to the worker who stood by the door.
4. Did you write the article that we were talking about?
5. Everyone is distressed by the kind of person that he has become.
6. They gave the movie which we saw a bad review.
7. The name that they called him was ridiculous.
8. The person to whom you should write is the manager.
9. She is a bore whom no one likes.
10. Anyone who laughs at me will be sorry.

C. Rewrite the following pairs of sentences as single sentences in which the second one is a relative clause embedded within the first:

> **example:**   a The sweater is old.
> b I gave her the sweater.
> The sweater that I gave her is old.

   1a. I wrote a poem.
    b. Everyone is laughing at my poem.
   2a. The key belongs to me.
    b. You found the key.
   3a. Someone threw a rock at the car.
    b. The car raced down the street.
   4a. I bought a new hat.
    b. I will not wear the new hat until next summer.
   5a. The river is now hazardous.
    b. We used to swim in the river.
   6a. The teacher began screaming.
    b. We drove the teacher crazy.
   7a. She opened the door for the man.
    b. The man was carrying a package.
   8a. The people seemed appreciative.
    b. We gave the tickets to the people.
   9a. Harold sneered at the poem.
    b. I had written the poem.
  10a. The house was insured.
    b. The house burned.

D. Explain why some of the following sentences are ungrammatical.
   Note: Some are correct.

   1. The girl which laughed made a fool of herself.
   2. Did you thank the man that gave you the quarter?
   3. Did you see the movie which I recommended?
   4. I don't like dogs who bark at me.
   5. The dog who greeted us at the door asked us to be seated.
   6. The book we were looking at has disappeared.
   7. The tree to which we walked was only a mile from the house.
   8. Did you see the man pushed you?
   9. The boy to I gave the dollar was grateful.
  10. The child the teacher scolded cried.

E. How many tests can you use to show that the italicized group of
   words in each of these sentences is or is not a noun phrase?

   1. *Those crimson sheets that you bought for your bed* shocked
      Martha.
   2. Harvey must have seen *the young man in the tuxedo last eve-
      ning*.

F. Rewrite each of the following sentences, changing the relative
   clauses to participial or prepositional phrases. Then tell what kind

of phrase each one is: present participial, past participial, or prepositional.

1. The boorish man who is sleeping on his back has begun to snore.
2. Did you cook the rooster that was hit by the truck?
3. He sent it to the student who is waiting outside.
4. Do those socks that are in the dryer belong to you?
5. The ham that was baked in the microwave oven was delicious.
6. Someone who was sitting in the front row was making rude noises.
7. He likes none of the people who are at work.
8. I handed the person who was in front of me a coupon.
9. Is she the woman who was shoved in front of a car?
10. The student who is writing his answers in red ink is in for a surprise.

G. Give the structure (relative clause, prepositional phrase, noun phrase, etc.) of each italicized group of words and tell how it functions (direct object, adverbial of time, modifier of *room*, etc.).

   examples: a. We gave *the child in the school yard* a ball.
   noun phrase–indirect object
   b. The man *by the tree* is a nuisance.
   prepositional phrase — modifies *man*

1. Harriet mailed the letter to her cousin *in Philadelphia*.
2. The plane will depart *at midnight*.
3. She has become *the most notorious woman in Canada*.
4. Those people *shivering by the fence* look cold.
5. The judges awarded the poem *submitted by Jack* first prize.
6. The program has been canceled because of a *wretched* mix up.
7. His *broken* arm prevented him from playing.
8. The trustees will appoint him *head librarian for the campus*.
9. Never has there been *a more egotistical person* than you.
10. *At the next corner* will you let me out?
11. *Who on earth* could it be?
12. He was in *the sitting room*.
13. I will help anyone *who asks for my assistance*.
14. The clouds *above* look threatening.
15. Is that your *leather* skirt?
16. Everywhere *we go* we see Judy.
17. Did you leave your shoes *outside*?
18. I could hardly stay on that *bucking* horse.

19. The *upstairs* offices are noisy.
20. I baked the cookies *you like so much.*

H. Write original sentences following the patterns given below:

1. Subject + Relative Clause − Verb − Predicate Noun
2. Time − Subject − Verb − Direct Object + Present Participial Phrase
3. Subject − Verb − Indirect Object + Prepositional Phrase − Direct Object
4. Subject + Past Participial Phrase − Verb − Predicate Adjective
5. Subject + Present Participial Phrase − Verb − Direct Object − Manner

I. The following passages have been written so that most noun modifiers appear in independent clauses. Revise them so that the sentences are less choppy and less important ideas are subordinated.

1. The lady laughed again. She was dark. They both relapsed upon the view. They were contemplating it in silence, and there was a sort of serenity. This serenity was diffused, and it might have been borrowed from the spring effulgence of the Roman skies.
2. The waiting room was not an inviting place. It was lit by the oil lamps, and they flared a red light over the benches. The red light was dull, and the benches were dingy.
3. But the Prince Prospero was happy and dauntless and sagacious. When his dominions were half depopulated, he summoned to his presence a thousand friends from among the knights and ladies of his court. These friends were hale and light-hearted. With them he retired to the seclusion of one of his abbeys. The seclusion was deep, and the abbey was castellated.
4. Hester Prynne went, one day, to the mansion of Governor Bellingham, with a pair of gloves. She had fringed and embroidered the gloves to his order, and they were to be worn on some great occasion of state.
5. On the other side he looked down into a mountain glen. It was deep, wild, lonely, and shagged. The bottom was filled with fragments from the cliffs. The cliffs were impending. The bottom was scarcely lighted by the rays of the sun. The rays were reflected, and the sun was setting.

8

Phrases and Clauses as Noun Phrases

The simplest kind of sentence is one with SVO order and a minimum number of words for each function:

> **8.1** My cousin saw a woman there.

We can easily recognize the subject, verb, direct object, and adverbial. With the addition of auxiliaries, we may expand the verb:

> **8.2** My cousin *must have seen* a woman there.

Or instead of a single-word adverbial, we may use a prepositional phrase:

> **8.3** My cousin must have seen a woman *at the carnival.*

Nouns may be modified by various structures, making them complex:

> **8.4** *My young cousin who is visiting me this week* must have seen a woman at the carnival.

121

8.5 My young cousin who is visiting me this week must have seen *a woman condemning smoking* at the carnival.

8.6 My young cousin who is visiting me this week must have seen a woman condemning smoking at *the carnival in the next county.*

Regardless of how far we expand each element, we still have the same basic structure as we did for **8.1:** subject, verb, direct object, adverbial of place.

A noun modifier may be a single word, such as an article, a possessive, a demonstrative, or an adjective, in which case it usually precedes the noun; or it may be a participial phrase or a relative clause, following the noun. There are various structures that modify nouns, but they all have the same function. If they are restrictive, their function is different from that of nonrestrictive modifiers.

NOUN CLAUSES

Instead of using a noun with modifiers to function as a subject, direct object, object of a preposition, and the like, we may use a *noun clause:*

8.7 Hiram believes [that he is right].

In this sentence the entire structure *that he is right* functions as the direct object of *believes,* as we can see if we substitute the pronoun *it* for the structure:

8.8 Hiram believes *it.*

The noun clause *that he is right* consists of the complete sentence *He is right,* to which the **conjunction** *that* has been attached. Unlike the relative pronoun *that,* the conjunction does not function as a subject, direct object, or the like.

Noun clauses may function in most of the ways that nouns do:

Subject

8.9a *This fact* is a shame.

   b [That you are ugly] is a shame.

Predicate Noun

8.10a The problem is *this.*

   b The problem is [that I've caught my hand in a jar].

Direct Object

8.11a   She knows *the answer.*

b   She knows [that you are the guilty one].

Except when the clause begins the sentence, *that* may be omitted:

8.12a   The answer was [that I was sick of her].

b   The answer was [I was sick of her].

8.13a   She said [that she was lucky].

b   She said [she was lucky].

At the beginning of the sentence, *that* may not be omitted:

8.14a   [That you will win the medal] seems unlikely.

b   *[You will win the medal] seems unlikely.

The reason for this restriction is that without *that* we have no way to recognize the structure as a noun clause. Therefore, we read *You will win the medal* as the main clause until we reach the verb *seems,* when we realize that something is wrong and go back. To avoid this kind of confusion, we always retain *that* when the clause comes at the beginning.

Subject noun clauses are often **extraposed** to the end of the sentence and their slot is filled with the **expletive** *it.* For example, we may have a sentence with a noun clause subject such as this:

8.15a   [That you are so indifferent] bothers me.

We may move the noun clause to the end:

8.15b   bothers me [that you are so indifferent].

Then, to fill the subject position, we add *it,* a word with no lexical meaning:

8.15c   *It* bothers me [that you are so indifferent].

Here are some additional examples of extraposed subject noun clauses:

8.16a   [That he will be on time] seems doubtful.

b   *It* seems doubtful [that he will be on time].

8.17a   [That you got caught in traffic] amused me.

b   *It* amused me [that you got caught in traffic].

In the **b** versions *that* may be omitted, because the noun clauses no longer come at the beginning of the sentence.

Although both the **a** and **b** versions of **8.16** and **8.17** are possible, those without extraposition seem somewhat formal. We extrapose subject noun clauses more often than we leave them in their basic position. At times, such as when the verb has nothing after it, extraposition is obligatory:

> **8.18a** *[That they are divorced] happens.
>
> **b** *It* happens [that they are divorced].
>
> **8.19a** *[That he is in a bad mood] appears.
>
> **b** *It* appears [that he is in a bad mood].

The **a** versions are not possible English sentences, as the asterisk indicates.

Some noun clauses function as ***appositives***. Let us first review this function with single nouns:

> **8.20** My friend *Jane* opened the package.
>
> **8.21** He went back to his home town, *Longview*.
>
> **8.22** He was talking to his neighbor, *an old grouch*.

In each instance, the appositive names the same subject as the noun preceding it. If it is restrictive, as in **8.20,** it gives a more precise name; that is, we assume that the speaker has more than one friend. *Jane* serves the function of limiting the class as an adjective would (e.g., *my oldest friend*). When the appositive is nonrestrictive, as in **8.21** and **8.22,** it does not restrict the noun it follows but rather gives more specific information about it. As the examples indicate, nonrestrictive appositives are set off with commas, but those that are restrictive are not. They follow the same principles as other restrictive and nonrestrictive elements, such as relative clauses.

Now let us look at noun clauses that function as appositives:

> **8.23** The assumption [that I will pay the bill] is faulty.
>
> **8.24** We considered the suggestion [that no one should go].
>
> **8.25** The fact [that we are learning a great deal] is obvious.

In each instance the noun clause gives a more specific statement of what the assumption, suggestion, or fact is. These are restrictive appositives.

Appositive noun clauses look a great deal like relative clauses, especially as both may begin with the word *that*. However, they can easily be shown to be quite different. First of all, they have a different semantic relationship to the noun they follow:

> **8.26** The suggestion [that he made] amused me.

8.27   The suggestion [that he should go] amused me.

In **8.26,** *that he made* is a relative clause. We do not know what the suggestion is but merely which one is being mentioned. In **8.27,** however, *that he should go* is an appositive, telling us specifically what the suggestion is.

As we look more closely at the two sentences, we see further differences. *That* in **8.26** is a relative pronoun, functioning as the object of *made*. Furthermore, it means *the suggestion.* As a relative pronoun, it can be replaced by *which:*

8.28   The suggestion [*which* he made] amused me.

In **8.27,** however, *that* has no lexical meaning; it merely serves to introduce the noun clause. And it does not have a syntactic function such as subject or object. It would be impossible to substitute *which* for it:

8.29   *The suggestion [*which* he should go] amused me.

Noun clauses beginning with *that* may look like relative clauses, but upon closer inspection we can see that they are different.

There is another structure that is even more difficult to classify. Grammarians in the past have not agreed on whether to call it a noun clause or a relative clause:

8.30   [What you said] bothered me.

8.31   I know [who brought the present].

8.32   She will give it to [whoever asks for it].

Because the structure can be replaced by a pronoun, we shall call it a noun clause, even though the meaning seems closer to that of a relative clause.

As with noun clauses beginning with *that,* those with WH words may function in most ways that nouns and pronouns do:

Subject

8.33   [Whatever you give him] will make him happy.

Direct Object

8.34   Betty believed [what you said].

Indirect Object

8.35   She will send [whoever answers the question] a prize.

Predicate Noun

8.36   That is not [what I said].

Objective Complement

8.37   I will call you [whatever I please].

Object of a Preposition

8.38   She will sit beside [whom she chooses].

These noun clauses are like relative clauses and questions in that they begin with a WH word that has been moved from its basic position in the sentence. We can illustrate this positioning by using the pronouns *something* and *someone* in the **a** versions below, where they are in their basic position; in the **b** versions they have been moved to the beginning and replaced with WH words:

8.39a   We read *something*.
   b   *what* we read
8.40a   *Someone* asks the first question.
   b   *whoever* asks the first question
8.41a   She gave *someone* the ticket.
   b   *whom* she gave the ticket

Like relative clauses, noun clauses can be paraphrased with complete sentences, and the WH words have specific functions such as subject or direct object within that sentence.

For those people who never use *whom,* there is no problem with which pronoun to use to represent humans; for those who follow the conventional practice of using *who* for subjects and predicate nouns and *whom* for all kinds of objects, it is essential to recognize how the pronoun is used within the noun clause. In the following sentence, for example, *who* is the subject of *sent:*

8.42   We know [*who* sent the money].

The entire noun clause is the object of *know,* as we can see if we replace it with a pronoun:

8.43   We know *that*.

If we substitute a noun for the pronoun *who,* converting the noun clause into a sentence, we readily see that it is the subject:

126

8.44a *who* sent the money

  b *Frank* sent the money.

When objects of prepositions are involved, either in the main or the noun clause, special care needs to be given to the structure:

8.45a We talked about [*who* would grade the papers].

  b We talked about *something.*

  c *Professor Horne* would grade the papers.

Whereas there may be some confusion as to what the object of *about* is in **8.45a,** if we substitute the pronoun *something* for the noun clause, as in **8.45b,** we see that the entire clause is the object of the preposition. Furthermore, if we replace *who* with a noun, as in **8.45c,** we see that it is the subject of *would grade.* Here is another example:

8.46a We know [about *whom* you are writing].

  b We know *something.*

  c You are writing about *Hans Hellmut Kirst.*

As we can see from the **b** and **c** versions, *about* is part of the noun clause, and the pronoun *whom* is its object.

It is possible to have more than one noun clause in a sentence, just as it is possible to have more than one relative clause. One way to do this is to let both subject and predicate noun be clauses:

8.47 [What I am trying to say] is [that this will not do].

Or we may add a noun clause within another one. For example, we may start with:

8.48a Grace thinks [that John believes something].

Instead of *something,* we may use a noun clause:

8.48b Grace thinks [that John believes [she told everyone something]].

Again, we may replace *something* with a noun clause:

8.48c Grace thinks [that John believes [she told everyone [that he thinks something]]].

Now that we have made our point, let us cut the sentence off with one more addition:

8.48d Grace thinks [that John believes [she told everyone [that he thinks [that he can fly]]]].

Such lengthy expansions become awkward and stylistically unpalatable, but we can theoretically continue them without limit.

When sentences containing noun clauses are turned into questions, the syntactic functions of all elements may not be immediately clear. For example, we may have a sentence such as this:

8.49a   He thinks [Albert will wash the car].

We can analyze the sentence without pausing. If we convert this into a yes–no question, we derive the following:

8.49b   Does he think [Albert will wash the car]?

Still there is no difficulty. However, if we turn this into a WH question, using an interrogative pronoun to replace *Albert,* we complicate the sentence:

8.49c   *Who* does he think [will wash the car]?

The subject of the noun clause has been moved to the beginning of the entire sentence. This arrangement plus the inverted word order *does he think* may make the function of *who* difficult for some people to determine. Here are some additional examples, in which related sentences are given without inversion:

8.50a   *Whom* did you say you saw?
    b   You said [you saw *Herman*].
8.51a   *Who* will she assume opened the bottle?
    b   She will assume [*I* opened the bottle].
8.52a   To *whom* do they believe we sent the money?
    b   They believe [we sent the money to *Virginia*].

The paraphrases clearly show how the interrogative pronouns function.

GERUND PHRASES

As we have seen, several different structures may function as subject, direct object, and the like:

Noun by Itself

8.53   *Sarah* startled everyone.

8.54 *The woman who was brushing her teeth in the restaurant* startled everyone.

Noun Clause with a **WH** Word

8.55 *What you did* startled everyone.

Noun Clause with **that**

8.56 It startled everyone *that you knew the answer.*

Pronoun

8.57 *She* startled everyone.

We can now add another structure, the ***gerund phrase:***

8.58 [Ann's opening the window] startled everyone.

A gerund phrase is formed from a sentence, as we can see by comparing the following versions:

8.59a Ann opened the window.

 b Ann's opening the window.

In both the sentence **a** and the gerund phrase **b**, *Ann* is the agent that performed the act of opening, and *the window* is the object that was affected by the action. The same subject-verb-object relationship is apparent in both. They differ in form in that the sentence contains tense, which is missing in the gerund phrase; for the latter, the subject is a possessive (*Ann's*), and the verb ends in *-ing* (*opening*).

A gerund phrase may function in many of the ways that a pronoun or other noun phrase does:

Subject

8.60a *It* amused me.

 b [Your losing your false teeth] amused me.

Direct Object

8.61a We enjoyed *it.*

b We enjoyed [Carl's telling us about his trip].

Predicate Noun

8.62a Our most boring moment was *that*.

b Our most boring moment was [his reciting that poem].

Object of a Preposition

8.63a We talked about *it*.

b We talked about [your leaving so early].

Indirect Object

8.64a We gave *it* no attention.

b We gave [your boasting] no attention.

As gerund phrases are derived from sentences, it is not surprising that they contain the same elements that sentences do. Here are a few examples:

Subject–Verb–Indirect Object–Direct Object

8.65a Paula handed Tom the script.

b Paula's handing Tom the script

Subject–Verb–Direct Object–Objective Complement

8.66a William left her alone.

b William's leaving her alone

Subject–Verb–Predicate Adjective

8.67a She looked frightened.

b her looking frightened

Subject–Verb–Adverbial of Time

8.68a He yelled during the lunch break.

b his yelling during the lunch break

Almost any sentence can be converted into a gerund phrase.

Whenever the subject of a gerund phrase names the same person or object that is mentioned in the main clause, it is deleted; that is, we have the **a** version below but not the **b:**

8.69a   Lois regretted [Karen's having seen the mess].

  b *Lois regretted [Lois' having seen the mess].

If we substitute a pronoun for the subject of the gerund, it cannot refer to *Lois:*

8.69c   Lois regretted [her having seen the mess].

If Lois is the one who saw the mess, we must use the following sentence:

8.69d   Lois regretted [having seen the mess].

That is, the subject of the gerund, though understood, does not appear. Here are some more examples:

8.70a   [Your having to eat and run] worried Agnes.

  b   [Having to eat and run] worried Agnes.

8.71a   They talked about [Paul's missing classes].

  b   They talked about [missing classes].

Whenever the subject of a gerund refers to the same individual or object as a noun phrase in the main sentence, it is deleted, as the **b** versions show; it is only when it refers to someone else, as in the **a** versions, that it remains.

There are other sentences in which the subject of a gerund is deleted, namely when it refers to people or things in general, as expressed by such indefinite pronouns as *one, someone, anyone, anything,* and the like.

8.72a   [One's being without a car] is a nuisance.

  b   [Being without a car] is a nuisance.

8.73a   The disagreeable feature is [someone's standing in the rain].

  b   The disagreeable feature is [standing in the rain].

After some verbs, indefinite objects are also deleted:

8.74a   [One's stealing something] is dishonest.

  b   [Stealing] is dishonest.

Even when a gerund phrase is reduced to a single word, as in **8.74b,** we still understand it as equivalent to a complete sentence with some of its elements deleted.

Because not all words that function as noun phrases and end in -*ing* are gerunds, let us see how we can distinguish them. First of all, gerunds are formed by adding the suffix -*ing* to verbs; therefore, such words as *spring, bring,* and *thing* are not gerunds, because *ing* is not a suffix. Similarly, certain proper nouns (*Browning, Reading*) are not gerunds. Nor are words formed by adding -*ing* to nouns: *siding, flooring, tubing, clothing.* None of these usually gives anyone trouble. But there are other words that do. *Painting* is a good example:

8.75a Those *paintings* will not sell.

  b *Painting* will ruin your clothes.

Although both uses of *painting* are derived from the verb *paint* plus the suffix -*ing,* only the **b** version is a gerund. The most reliable test is to see whether it corresponds to a sentence or not. We understand **8.75b** to mean *You paint something,* but **8.75a** has no such meaning. In fact, we could substitute another noun, such as *objects,* for *paintings* in **8.75a,** but not for a gerund. Additionally, nouns may be pluralized or preceded by articles and demonstratives; gerunds may not. Here are a few additional examples, with nouns in the **a** versions and gerunds in **b:**

8.76a Each *warning* made me more cautious.

  b His *warning* me about the consequences made me more cautious.

8.77a Have you read her *writings?*

  b I regretted her *writing* that letter.

8.78a She gave me a good *hugging.*

  b *Hugging* strangers will get you into trouble.

Although such words as *warning, writing, hugging,* and the like may function either as gerunds or as nouns, the two uses are clearly different.

Gerunds and present participles are two other structures that look alike, and both are derived from verbs:

8.79 [Reading the gas meter] is not very exciting.

8.80 The man [reading the gas meter] is not very exciting.

These structures are derived from *one reads the gas meter* and *the man is reading the gas meter,* respectively. Whereas both appear as *reading the gas meter,* we can see that the structure in **8.79** functions as a gerund phrase; it is the subject of *is* and can be replaced with a pronoun such as *it.* In **8.80,** however, *reading the gas meter* is a participial phrase that modifies *the man.* Participial phrases can always be paraphrased with relative clauses:

8.81 The man [who is reading the gas meter] is not very exciting.

Sometimes a sentence is ambiguous, depending upon whether the *-ing* word functions as a gerund or as a participle:

8.82 [Hitting strangers] might be dangerous.

We can understand *strangers* as the object of *hitting* or as a noun modified by a participle.

INFINITIVE PHRASES

There is another structure that can function as a noun phrase: the *infinitive phrase.*

8.83a [For Julia to become ill] would surprise everyone.

We can compare this structure with the gerund phrase:

8.83b [Julia's becoming ill] would surprise everyone.

Like the gerund phrase, an infinitive does not contain tense. The subject is preceded by the preposition *for,* and the verb is preceded by the word *to.* Both of the above phrases are related to the following sentence:

8.83c Julia becomes ill.

The sentence has tense, and it does not contain any of the markers of the gerund (possessive, *-ing*) or of the infinitive (*for, to*). Yet in all three we recognize *Julia* as the subject of *become* and *ill* as a predicate adjective.

An infinitive phrase can function in almost all the ways other noun phrases do:

Subject

8.84a [For you to make a generous contribution] would please me very much.

b It would please me very much [for you to make a generous contribution].

Direct Object

8.85 She said [for Caleb to shut his mouth].

8.86   The solution is [for you to appear bored].

As we see in **8.84b,** infinitive phrases used as subjects can be extraposed, just as noun clauses can. Also, since infinitive phrases are derived from sentences, they may contain any of the elements found in a sentence, such as subject, direct object, predicate adjective, and so on.

As is true with the gerund phrase, the subject of an infinitive phrase is deleted if it refers to the same person or object as a noun phrase in the main sentence:

8.87   It would disturb Henry [for you to pay the bill].

8.88a   *It would disturb Henry [for Henry to pay the bill].

   b   It would disturb Henry [to pay the bill].

Although the subject of *pay* is not expressed overtly in **8.88b,** it is clearly understood.

Also, indefinite subjects and objects of infinitives are often deleted:

8.89a   [For someone to read something] is [for someone to live vicariously].

   b   [To read] is [to live vicariously].

As a result of deletion, all that is left of the infinitive phrase is often just the infinitive itself. Note, however, that we understand all elements of the sentence.

After prepositions and after certain verbs, the *to* of the infinitive does not appear:

8.90   We did everything except *cry.*

8.91   He did nothing but *stand* there and look frightened.

8.92   We let Harold *do* it.

8.93   She made her mother *burn* the trash.

Otherwise these infinitives are like all others.

PHRASES, CLAUSES, AND SENTENCES

We have now seen three kinds of phrases and two types of dependent clauses that share certain features with sentences. Let us review them. First we noticed that all these structures contain the basic elements — subject, verb, complement, and optional adverbial:

8.94 The neighbors painted their house brown yesterday. (sentence containing subject–verb–direct object–objective complement–adverbial of time)

8.95 Did you know [that the neighbors painted their house brown yesterday]? (noun clause containing the same elements as the sentence)

8.96 The neighbors [who painted their house brown yesterday] aren't very friendly. (relative clause containing the same elements as the sentence, the subject represented as a relative pronoun)

8.97 I was amused by [the neighbors' painting their house brown yesterday]. (gerund phrase)

8.98 The neighbors, [painting their house brown yesterday], were unable to go to the meeting. (present participial phrase)

8.99 I didn't expect [the neighbors to paint their house brown yesterday]. (infinitive phrase)

Whatever the structure, we recognize *the neighbors* as the subject, *painted* as the verb, *their house* as the direct object, *brown* as an objective complement, and *yesterday* as an adverbial of time. In the three phrases the verb does not show tense, and it is altered according to the kind of phrase in which it occurs: with the *-ing* suffix (*painting*) in the gerund and present participial phrases and preceded by *to* (*to paint*) in the infinitive phrase. We also find variation in the subject: It is represented with a relative pronoun (*who*) in the relative clause; it is a possessive (*the neighbors'*) in the gerund phrase; and it is deleted in the present participial phrase. We nevertheless understand the same subject as we do for the sentence **8.94.**

Unlike sentences, phrases often have their subjects deleted. Participial phrases always do, and gerund and infinitive phrases do if the subject renames a noun phrase in the main clause or if it is an indefinite pronoun:

8.100a She deplored [your hitchhiking].

b She deplored [hitchhiking].

In the **a** version we see the subject *your* expressed because it does not refer to a noun phrase in the main clause and it is not an indefinite pronoun. In the **b** sentence, however, there is no subject expressed for the gerund because it is either *her* or *someone's*.

We can find other features of sentences within dependent clauses and phrases. A verb in any of them may be intransitive:

8.101   The tree fell to the ground.

8.102   He said [that the tree fell to the ground].

8.103   The tree [that fell to the ground] was old.

8.104   [The tree's falling to the ground] upset me.

8.105   The tree [falling to the ground] is my favorite.

8.106   He watched [the tree fall to the ground].

Or it may be transitive, taking a direct object:

8.107a   The man caught the dog.

8.108a   It amused me [that the man caught the dog].

8.109a   Did you recognize the man [who caught the dog]?

8.110a   I talked about [the man's catching the dog].

8.111a   We laughed at the man [catching the dog].

8.112a   It would be absurd [for the man to catch the dog].

Like other transitive verbs, these may become passives:

8.107b   The dog was caught by the man.

8.108b   It amused me [that the dog was caught by the man].

8.109b   Did you recognize the dog [that was caught by the man]?

8.110b   I talked about [the dog's being caught by the man].

8.111b   We laughed at the dog [caught by the man].

8.112b   It would be absurd [for the dog to be caught by the man].

Some transitive verbs take indirect objects, and others take objective complements. Still other verbs are linking, taking predicate nouns or predicate adjectives.

These five clauses and phrases differ among themselves in the ways they function. Relative clauses and participial phrases modify nouns:

8.113a   We passed by the man [who was thumbing a ride].

b   We passed by the man [thumbing a ride].

8.114   The coat [burned in the fire] wasn't mine.

Noun clauses, gerund phrases, and infinitive phrases function as noun phrases:

8.115a   He knows *it*.

b   He knows [that you did it].

8.116a   *It* was a mistake.

b   [His leaving early] was a mistake.

8.117a I like *it*.

    b I like [to sleep late].

At first these structures may appear complicated. When we realize that they share the same features and functions as the elements of simple sentences, they become much easier to analyze.

EXERCISES

A. Enclose the noun clauses in brackets and tell how they function (subject, direct object, etc.):

    1. Your silly mother thinks that this bland meal is good.
    2. It is horrible that you won't help us.
    3. His reason is that he can't stand you.
    4. Did he tell whoever was sitting beside him the answer?
    5. He will hand it to whomever he selects.
    6. Did she tell you to whom she will send the letter?
    7. That you are guilty is obvious.
    8. He names his cars whatever he chooses.
    9. Everyone is saying that you are lying.
    10. It pleased us that she was so cautious.

B. Classify the italicized structures as noun clauses or relative clauses and provide evidence for your answers:

    1. The belief *that John cheated* is appalling.
    2. The belief *that John suggested* is appalling.
    3. The suggestion *that we should wait* is agreeable.
    4. We disregarded the fact *that it was raining*.
    5. We disregarded the fact *that he pointed out*.

C. Fill in the blanks with *who* or *whom,* according to the rules for formal English, and tell how each pronoun functions (direct object, predicate pronoun, etc.):

    1. _____ did she think it was?
    2. _____ are you looking for?
    3. _____ would you say stole the money?
    4. Arnold asked them _____ their sister married.
    5. Billy told them _____ had helped him.
    6. Is there any question as to _____ will succeed them?
    7. The Secretary of State is the man _____ they believe is responsible for the problem.
    8. Our helping you will depend upon _____ you pay.

9. Your winning the election will depend upon _____ your supporters are.
10. _____ do you think Kathy said the stranger was?

D. Enclose the gerund phrases in brackets and tell how they function:

1. Curt's smoking his pipe in the elevator made us sick.
2. Paul despises riding buses.
3. Are you afraid of flying?
4. Ellen must have given practicing Chopin her full attention.
5. We were talking about the folly of paying one's debts.
6. Donna's skating was amusing.
7. She must loathe repeating her name all the time.
8. Our favorite pastime is working crossword puzzles.
9. Counting sheep won't make anyone fall asleep.
10. I found cleaning ovens rather exciting work.

E. Enclose the infinitive phrases in brackets and tell how they function:

1. Harry said for Perry to stop cheating.
2. Their greatest ambition is to retire early.
3. It is easy to insult them.
4. I could do nothing except cough.
5. To know that you are right is not enough.
6. It is silly for you to wait any longer.
7. He hoped to arrive early.
8. Their plan was for Bill to wash the car.

F. Paraphrase the infinitive and gerund phrases in the last two exercises as complete sentences.

   example: Victoria wanted [to open the package herself].
                  Victoria opened the package herself.

G. Classify the italicized words as verbs, gerunds, nouns, participles, adjectives, or parts of compounds:

1. We enjoyed *running*.
2. We were *running* to the door.
3. We watched the *running* man.
4. That was a *puzzling* answer.
5. I enjoyed the *writings* that he let me read.
6. I disapproved of his *writing* the letter himself.
7. It was a *breeding* ground for mosquitoes.
8. She wore a *charming* smile.
9. He calls *writing* poetry fun.
10. He let the *sleeping* dogs lie.

11. That *infuriating* man is at the door again.
12. I gave them my *blessing*.
13. He tried to catch the *praying* mantis.
14. *Rolling* stones gather no moss.
15. *Rolling* stones is boring work.
16. I sent her a *greeting* card.
17. They were *greeting* us at the door.
18. *Greeting* people at the door is polite.
19. The man *greeting* the guests is not the host.
20. Your *greetings* do not sound sincere.

H. Classify each italicized group of words as to structure (gerund phrase, noun clause, etc.) and function (direct object, modifier, etc.):

1. We thought *that the refrigerator needed repairs.*
2. The members were talking about *inviting her to the next meeting.*
3. Did you send the people *waiting in line* enough tickets?
4. It upset me *that he laughed at my lisp.*
5. The candidate *wearing the dark coat* will probably win.
6. I believe *you are the cutest thing in town.*
7. The guest slept in the *freshly painted* bedroom.
8. *Gerald's reaching for the butter* amused everyone.
9. He did everything but *jump over the moon.*
10. Any car *that I buy* will have to be cheap.
11. *Taking cold showers* is good for the circulation.
12. It seems risky *for you to reduce so fast.*
13. I ignored the noises *they were making.*
14. The fact *that we are poor* disturbs us.
15. The fact *that upset us the most* was our poverty.
16. It is pleasant *to be praised.*
17. The people *between whom I sat* were unfriendly.
18. He enjoys *bragging about himself.*
19. We scoffed at the man *bragging about himself.*
20. Would you like *to walk barefoot over glass?*

I. Each of the following sentences is ambiguous because a word or phrase can be interpreted as being more than one structure. Explain.

1. The thought that he had proposed disturbed Emma.
2. That prim grandmother detests smoking cigars.
3. Kissing neighbors can be fun.
4. You are too big to push.

J. Write original sentences containing the following structures:

1. Noun clause introduced with *that* functioning as subject (extraposed)
2. Noun clause introduced with a WH word functioning as subject (not extraposed)
3. Noun clause introduced with *that* functioning as direct object
4. Noun clause introduced with a WH word functioning as object of a preposition
5. Gerund phrase functioning as subject
6. Gerund phrase functioning as indirect object
7. Infinitive phrase functioning as extraposed subject
8. Infinitive phrase functioning as direct object

9

Movable Modifiers

In the last eight chapters we have examined two general types of syntactic relationships: subject–verb–complement structures and structures of modification. As examples of the first, we talked about the kinds of words that may function as subjects and complements, and we noticed various complements:

> **9.1** The barrel is empty. (subject–verb–predicate adjective)
>
> **9.2** They became believers. (subject–verb–predicate noun)
>
> **9.3** The doorman pushed the cart. (subject–verb–direct object)

We also looked at sentences containing indirect objects, appositives, and objective complements.

We saw further that we could embed a sentence into a noun-phrase position:

> **9.4a** Larry believes [something]. He will be elected.
>
> **b** Larry believes [that he will be elected].

9.5a We talked about [something]. You spied on Terry.

  b We talked about [your spying on Terry].

9.6a [Something] would be disastrous. Tommy tells about his plan.

  b [For Tommy to tell about his plan] would be disastrous.

  c It would be disastrous [for Tommy to tell about his plan].

In **9.4a** *something* functions as the direct object; the noun clause *that he will be elected* has the same function in **9.4b**. Both *something* and the gerund phrase *your spying on Terry* are objects of the preposition *about* in **9.5**. In **9.6** the pronoun *something* and the infinitive phrase *for Tommy to tell about his plan* function as subjects. In **9.6c** this phrase has been extraposed. Various kinds of structures may function as subjects and complements.

As for structures of modification, we saw two types. One of these is the adjectival, which can be a single word, a phrase, or a clause:

9.7 We watched the *dark* clouds. (single-word adjective)

9.8 He whistled a tune [that sounded familiar]. (relative clause)

9.9 Those people [staring at the moon] missed your stunt. (present participial phrase)

In addition, there are past participial phrases and prepositional phrases that modify nouns.

The other kind of modifier is the adverbial, either a single word or a prepositional phrase:

9.10a Henry left for school *yesterday*. (single-word adverb)

9.11a She opened the package *with great delight*. (prepositional phrase)

Some adverbial modifiers may be shifted to the beginning of the sentence:

9.10b *Yesterday* Henry left for school.

9.11b *With great delight,* she opened the package.

The positioning of such adverbial modifiers usually depends upon our concern for sentence variety and emphasis. In this chapter we shall examine a number of other modifiers that may be moved to various positions and show how this rearrangement affects the reader's ability to grasp the subject–verb–complement structure of the sentence.

ADVERB CLAUSES

In addition to single-word adverbs and prepositional phrases, there are *adverb clauses* that function as adverbials of manner, time, place, and the like. Let us start with adverbials of time:

9.12 The doorbell rang *yesterday*. (single-word adverb)

9.13 The doorbell rang *at six o'clock*. (prepositional phrase)

9.14 The doorbell rang [while I was cutting my nails]. (adverb clause)

Like other adverbials, adverb clauses can designate time in various ways:

9.15 They laughed [when they saw her expression]. (single point in time)

9.16 He tries to trip me [whenever I pass his desk]. (habitual action)

The time of the action or state in the adverb clause may be different from that of the main clause:

9.17 They had already left [before we arrived].

9.18 They left [after we arrived].

Like single-word adverbs and prepositional phrases, adverb clauses that designate time can be replaced with *then* and questioned with *when:*

9.19a They became bored [when we showed the home movies].

b They became bored *then*.

c *When* did they become bored?

All adverbials of time—single-word adverbs, prepositional phrases, and adverb clauses—function alike. They differ only in structure.

To form an adverb clause, we add a subordinating conjunction to a sentence. Hence, we merely add a word such as *when, before, after, if,* and the like to the sentence *I fell* to produce any of the following adverb clauses: *when I fell, after I fell, before I fell, until I fell.* The list of subordinating conjunctions is longer than that of some other elements such as relative pronouns, but we can learn to recognize them easily through examples.

Just as single-word adverbs and prepositional phrases serve functions other than that of time adverbial, adverb clauses have other uses:

Place

9.20 They are still [where I left them].

9.21 I will sit [wherever I choose].

Manner

9.22 He announced the guest [as we had told him to].

9.23 Cathy smiled [as though she recognized us].

Reason

9.24 They sold the washing machine [because they are moving].

There are also several functions of adverb clauses that have no counterparts in single-word adverbs or prepositional phrases:

Condition

9.25 I'll scream [if you say another word].

9.26 They won't come [unless you invite them].

Concession

9.27 Harriet finished the race [although she had trouble].

9.28 We will go [even if it is raining].

We could easily extend this list of types of adverb clauses, but our intention is to illustrate them for recognition purposes.

In Chapter 2, we saw that single-word adverbs and prepositional phrases can be moved to the beginning of the sentence for variety or emphasis. Adverb clauses may also be fronted:

9.29a I will try to help [if you tell me what is wrong].

b [If you tell me what is wrong], I will try to help.

9.30a They had fled [before we could catch them].

b [Before we could catch them], they had fled.

9.31a I am moving to another room [because you are annoying me].

b [Because you are annoying me], I am moving to another room.

144

Unless they are very short, introductory adverb clauses are followed by commas.

ABSOLUTE PHRASES

Similar in meaning to the adverb clause is the structure known as the *absolute phrase:*

9.32a [If the weather permits], we can sleep outdoors tonight. (adverb clause)

b [The weather permitting], we can sleep outdoors tonight. (absolute phrase)

9.33a [Because her skirt was caught on a nail], she could not move. (adverb clause)

b [Her skirt caught on a nail], she could not move. (absolute phrase)

In form, an absolute phrase looks like a participial phrase that has a subject; we notice the present participle *permitting* in **9.32b,** the past participle *caught* in **9.33b.**

Absolute phrases may contain participles or any other structure that follows *be:*

9.34a [The floor being wet and slippery], we stayed outside.

b [The floor wet and slippery], we stayed outside.

9.35a [The answers being on the blackboard], we felt more confident than before.

b [The answers on the blackboard], we felt more confident than before.

Whenever a participle is not present, *being* is understood as part of the absolute phrase; we can say, therefore, that an absolute phrase consists of a subject and a participial phrase, either past or present. Like other participial phrases, this one can be active or passive, transitive or intransitive, and so on. It differs from a verb in that it does not contain tense.

Just as adverb clauses may be found at the beginning or the end of the sentence, absolute phrases may occur at either place:

9.36a [Bob having already left in the car], Carol and I walked.

b Carol and I walked, [Bob having already left in the car].

9.37a   [His voice drowned out by the noise], the speaker interrupted his lecture.

b   The speaker interrupted his lecture, [his voice drowned
out by the noise].

9.38a   [There being nothing else we could do], we laughed.

b   We laughed, [there being nothing else we could do].

The choice of position depends upon emphasis and variety, not meaning.

INFINITIVE PHRASES AS ADVERBIALS

In addition to adverb clauses, absolute phrases, adverbs, and prepositional phrases, we find some infinitive phrases functioning as adverbials:

9.39a   Hank came to the party [so that he could see Judy]. (adverb clause)

b   Hank came to the party [to see Judy]. (infinitive phrase)

9.40a   Lorraine put on her glasses [so that she could see better].
(adverb clause)

b   Lorraine put on her glasses [to see better]. (infinitive
phrase)

As with other infinitive phrases, we understand a subject that refers to
the same person mentioned in the main clause; that is, we understand
Hank as subject of *to see Judy* in **9.39b** and *Lorraine* as subject in **9.40b**.

Some infinitive phrases cannot be paraphrased with adverb
clauses, as we can see in the following sentences:

9.41   Thelma looked up suddenly [to find a cat on the chair].

9.42   What can I do [to make you happy]?

9.43   He stopped smoking only [to start again].

These infinitive phrases are different from those in **9.39–9.40** in that
we do not ask questions about them. For **9.39b** and **9.40b,** we have the
following questions:

9.39c   Why did Hank come to the party?

9.40c   Why did Lorraine put on her glasses?

There are no questions like these for **9.41–9.43.**

Another difference between the infinitive phrases in **9.39–9.40** and those in **9.41–9.43** is that the former, but not the latter, may be fronted:

9.39d [To see Judy], Hank came to the party.

9.40d [To see better], Lorraine put on her glasses.

If we fronted the infinitive phrase in **9.41,** we would change the meaning:

9.44 [To find a cat on her chair], Thelma looked up suddenly.

This sentence means that Thelma's *purpose* for looking up was to find a cat on her chair, whereas **9.41** suggests that she was not deliberately looking for a cat. Her looking up merely resulted in her seeing one. Only those infinitive phrases that can be paraphrased as adverb clauses may be moved to the front of the sentence.

FRONTED NOUN MODIFIERS

Certain noun modifiers may also be moved to the beginning of the sentence when they are nonrestrictive:

Present Participial Phrase

9.45a Louis, [opening the door to the stable], let the horse out.

   b [Opening the door to the stable], Louis let the horse out.

9.46a Mr. Phillips, [not knowing what else to do], sat on his hands.

   b [Not knowing what else to do], Mr. Phillips sat on his hands.

Past Participial Phrase

9.47a The dentist, [caught by surprise], let the receptionist help him.

   b [Caught by surprise], the dentist let the receptionist help him.

9.48a My grandmother, [attacked by a pack of angry children], screamed for help.

b   [Attacked by a pack of angry children], my grandmother screamed for help.

Appositive of Two or More Words

9.49a   The sea captain, [an old hand at these matters], knew instantly what was wrong with the sail.

b   [An old hand at these matters], the sea captain knew instantly what was wrong with the sail.

9.50a   Janice, [an especially energetic student], volunteered to give the report.

b   [An especially energetic student], Janice volunteered to give the report.

Adjective with Modifiers

9.51a   The baby, [sick with a cold], cried all night.

b   [Sick with a cold], the baby cried all night.

9.52a   Helen, [blue from the freezing wind], could say nothing.

b   [Blue from the freezing wind], Helen could say nothing.

These modifiers are always followed by commas when they are placed at the beginning of the sentence.

Modifiers such as those in sentences **9.45–9.52** usually describe the subject. If they are intended to modify other words, we call them *dangling modifiers.* The **a** versions below are acceptable, but the modifiers in the **b** sentences are dangling:

9.53a   Running from the burning building, Sophie carried the paralyzed child.

b   Running from the burning building, the paralyzed child was carried by Sophie.

9.54a   Pleased with the paper, the teacher congratulated Mark.

b   Pleased with the paper, Mark was congratulated by the teacher.

9.55a   Caught in a trap, the beaver was found by the hunter.

b   Caught in a trap, the hunter found the beaver.

Some dangling modifiers produce grotesque or confused results; others are just clumsy. Even when the meaning is clear, they are usually avoided by good writers.

EXTRAPOSED NOUN MODIFIERS

In Chapter 8 we saw that subject noun clauses are often extraposed to the end of the sentence:

9.56a [That you are so peculiar] bothers me.

b It bothers me [that you are so peculiar].

We may extrapose relative clauses in the same manner:

9.57a There was a woman [whose name was Heather] standing there.

b There was a woman standing there [whose name was Heather].

9.58a They said something [that I didn't appreciate] to him.

b They said something to him [that I didn't appreciate].

Here are examples of other noun modifiers that have been extraposed:

Appositive

9.59a The realization [that she might be the murderer] suddenly hit me.

b The realization suddenly hit me [that she might be the murderer].

9.60a I was robbed of $256, [a sum I could hardly afford to lose], by the burglar.

b I was robbed of $256 by the burglar, [a sum I could hardly afford to lose].

Present Participial Phrase

9.61a Annette, [looking for her uncle's Pontiac], watched every car that passed.

b Annette watched every car that passed, [looking for her uncle's Pontiac].

9.62a They, [not caring whom they might hurt], dropped bricks onto the sidewalk.

b They dropped bricks onto the sidewalk, [not caring whom they might hurt].

149

Past Participial Phrase

9.63a Carl, [stunned by the news], stood still.

   b Carl stood still, [stunned by the news].

9.64a Bob, [pushed by an unknown stranger who was lurking in the shadows], fell in front of the car.

   b Bob fell in front of the car, [pushed by an unknown stranger who was lurking in the shadows].

Adjective of Two or More Words

9.65a My car, [shiny after the waxing], stood in the driveway.

   b My car stood in the driveway, [shiny after the waxing].

9.66a Richard, [afraid to trust anyone], kept quiet.

   b Richard kept quiet, [afraid to trust anyone].

When these modifiers are long, they are usually fronted or extraposed.

THE PLACEMENT OF MODIFIERS

So far we have said little about why we move a modifier to the beginning or end of a sentence. As we look at sentences written by various authors, we can recognize a number of circumstances that may make one position preferable to another.

Good writers usually try to avoid a series of sentences that begin with the same structure unless they are being deliberately abrupt. To break up the monotony of a number of sentences beginning with subject plus verb, they look for other structures to begin some of their sentences. The following passage from "Tennessee's Partner" by Bret Harte illustrates varied sentence beginnings. During Tennessee's trial, his partner comes into the courtroom and offers the jury $1700 to let Tennessee go free. Then follows this paragraph:

> For a moment his life was in jeopardy. One or two men sprang to their feet, several hands groped for hidden weapons, and a suggestion to "throw him from the window" was only overridden by a gesture from the Judge. Tennessee laughed. And apparently oblivious of the excitement, Tennessee's Partner improved the opportunity to mop his face again with his handkerchief.

The first sentence provides a general statement about the effect of the attempted bribery. The sentences that follow describe the specific

150

actions of various people in the room. To indicate the tension, Harte begins the sentences describing the actions with the subject in each case. By starting the first sentence with a prepositional phrase, he sets it apart and prevents the overuse of sentences with initial subjects. After the opening sentence we find the following series of events:

1. One or two men sprang to their feet.
2. Several hands groped for hidden weapons.
3. A suggestion to "throw him from the window" was only overridden by a gesture from the Judge.
4. Tennessee laughed.
5. And apparently oblivious of the excitement, Tennessee's Partner improved the opportunity to mop his face again with his handkerchief.

We might ask why Harte did not begin the last sentence with the subject because the *and* makes it look like the last item in a series:

And Tennessee's Partner improved the opportunity to mop his face again with his handkerchief, apparently oblivious of the excitement.

Such a revision would not have been effective. The sequence of related actions actually culminates with the crisp "Tennessee laughed." The partner wipes his face, not as an act prompted by the others, but as one of apparent lack of awareness. By using different kinds of beginnings for the first and last sentences, Harte has set them off from the internal sentences. This use of sentence variety is an aid to establishing the meaning of the paragraph, not just a breaking of monotony.

A second reason for fronting an adverbial modifier is to emphasize parallel or contrasting ideas. In Steinbeck's *Of Mice and Men* we find the following:

Crooks sat on his bunk. His shirt was out of his jeans in back. In one hand he held a bottle of liniment, and with the other he rubbed his spine.

The last sentence could as easily have been written, "He held a bottle of liniment in one hand, and he rubbed his spine with the other," but the contrast between "in one hand" and "with the other" would have been weakened. Similarly, in *The Old Man and the Sea,* Hemingway wrote the following paragraph:

On this circle the old man could see the fish's eye and the two gray sucking fish that swam around him. Sometimes they attached themselves to him. Sometimes they darted off. Sometimes they would swim easily in his shadow. They were each over three feet long and when they swam fast they lashed their whole bodies like eels.

The three sentences beginning with *sometimes* could have had the adverb moved to the end or between the subject and the verb, but placed at the beginning it emphasizes the parallel sentences that describe related actions.

If an adverb clause contains a pronoun or other transitional word referring to a word in a previous sentence, it is usually placed first. For example, one paragraph in Oliver Goldsmith's *The Vicar of Wakefield* ends with the landlord's departure:

> At the approach of evening he took his leave; but not till he had requested permission to renew his visit, which, as he was our landlord, we most readily agreed to.

The next paragraph then begins,

> As soon as he was gone, my wife called a council on the conduct of the day.

By placing the adverb clause first, Goldsmith let the pronoun *he* come close to its antecedent. Because this clause serves as a transition between paragraphs, it is appropriately placed first. Other transitional phrases such as *in the first place* and *on the other hand* often come at the beginning of the sentence.

In other sentences we avoid ambiguity by positioning a phrase or clause in one position rather than another:

> **9.67a**   He watched the fugitive [as he moved forward].
>
> **b**   [As he moved forward], he watched the fugitive.

In **9.67a,** the second *he* could refer to the first *he* or to *the fugitive;* in the **b** version there is no confusion. Another kind of ambiguity results from adverbials that may modify an embedded sentence or the main sentence:

> **9.68a**   Harold read the note you gave him on the bus.

Did he read the note on the bus, or did you give it to him there? That is, which of the following structures is intended?

> **9.68b**   Harold read the note [you gave him] on the bus.
>
> **c**   Harold read the note [you gave him on the bus].

If we want to state where the reading took place, we can easily move the prepositional phrase to the beginning:

9.68d   On the bus, Harold read the note you gave him.

There is no longer any ambiguity.

Another factor affecting the placement of modifiers is length. As long as subject, verb, complement, and adverbial are all short, there is no problem recognizing the structure, wherever the adverbial is placed:

9.69a   Patty leaves for India *tomorrow.*

   b   Patty leaves *tomorrow* for India.

   c   *Tomorrow,* Patty leaves for India.

On the other hand, if any of these elements are long, their length may affect our freedom in positioning them. For example, here is how Coleridge could have written one of his sentences in *Biographia Literaria:*

> When the sonnets of Mr. Bowles, twenty in number, and just then published in a quarto pamphlet, were first made known and presented to me, by a schoolfellow who had quitted us for the university and who, during the whole time that he was in our first form (or in our school language, a Grecian) had been my patron and protector, I had just entered on my seventeenth year.

Because of the length of the adverb clause ("When ... protector"), most readers flounder before they come to the main clause: "I had just entered on my seventeenth year." When the adverb clause comes last, the sentence is fairly easy to understand:

> I had just entered on my seventeenth year when the sonnets of Mr. Bowles, twenty in number, and just then published in a quarto pamphlet, were first made known and presented to me, by a schoolfellow who had quitted us for the university and who, during the whole time that he was in our first form (or in our school language, a Grecian) had been my patron and protector.

This, of course, is the way Coleridge wrote the sentence. After reading the short main clause, we know what the structure is and can relax while we let the adverb clause unfold. In the first version we keep asking ourselves where the introductory modifier ends.

At times it is the length of the complement rather than that of the adverbial that influences the word order, as we can see from a sentence in Charles Lamb's essay "Christ's Hospital Five and Thirty Years Ago":

In Mr. Lamb's *Works*, published a year or two since, I find a magnificent eulogy on my old school, such as it was, or now appears to him to have been, between the years 1782 and 1789.

If the phrase "In Mr. Lamb's *Works*, published a year or two since" had been placed at the end of the sentence, the meaning would have been hazy because of the long, complex direct object.

Length can also influence the word order for noun modifiers. As long as all elements are fairly short, we have no trouble understanding the structure regardless of where certain modifiers are positioned:

9.70a Paul, [holding his hand over his nose], ran from the room.

   b [Holding his hand over his nose], Paul ran from the room.

   c Paul ran from the room, [holding his hand over his nose].

However, when the modifier is longer, its position may affect the intelligibility of the sentence, as we can see from a passage in Hawthorne's "Young Goodman Brown." The first sentence is provided as a context.

Young Goodman Brown came forth at sunset into the street at Salem village; but put his head back, after crossing the threshold, to exchange a parting kiss with his young wife. And Faith, as the wife was aptly named, thrust her own pretty head into the street, letting the wind play with the pink ribbons of her cap while she called to Goodman Brown.

The participial phrase "letting the wind ... Goodman Brown" has been extraposed for a good reason, as we can see from a revision in which it follows the subject:

And Faith, as the wife was aptly named, letting the wind play with the pink ribbons of her cap while she called to Goodman Brown, thrust her own pretty head into the street.

By the time we get to the end of the modifier, we have lost track of the structure. Good writers try to avoid arrangements of elements that make sentence structures difficult to grasp.

Finally, when a pronoun naming a specific individual has a modifier, this modifier is usually extraposed or placed at the beginning of the sentence:

9.71a He, [ignoring our words of caution], went into the unlighted alley.

   b [Ignoring our words of caution], he went into the unlighted alley.

    c   He went into the unlighted alley, [ignoring our words of caution].

The first version is clumsier than the other two. It should be noted that this restriction involves only pronouns referring to specific individuals. Generic pronouns — those naming people in general — have their modifiers immediately following them:

    9.72   He [who wants to succeed] must work hard.

Otherwise, personal pronouns usually are not followed immediately by modifiers.

    At times it is an author's sense of rhythm or style that dictates the placement of a movable modifier. However, the reasons given above for choosing one position over another are the ones most frequently considered.

EXERCISES

A. From the paragraph from Joseph Conrad's *The Secret Agent* given below, find an example of each of the following structures:

1. transitive verb	7. absolute phrase
2. intransitive verb	8. past participial phrase
3. linking verb	9. present participial phrase
4. coordinate adjectives	10. adverbial of manner
5. adjective ending in *-ed*	11. gerund phrase
6. compound noun	12. appositive

It was not a long drive. It ended by signal abruptly, nowhere in particular, between two lamp-posts before a large drapery establishment — a long range of shops already lapped up in sheets of corrugated iron for the night. Tendering a coin through the trap door, the fare slipped out and away, leaving an effect of uncanny eccentric ghostliness upon the driver's mind. But the size of the coin was satisfactory to his touch, and his education not being literary, he remained untroubled by the fear of finding it presently turned to a dead leaf in his pocket. Raised above the world of fares by the nature of his calling, he contemplated their action with a limited interest. The sharp pulling of his horse right round expressed his philosophy.

B. Some of the following sentences contain dangling modifiers. Revise them, but do nothing to the others.

    1. Driving through the slush, the weather seemed worse than ever.

2. Being just a teenager, his father did not let him drink cocktails.
3. After coaxing, he decided to go.
4. The program was canceled after examining the small number of advance ticket sales.
5. To succeed on the driving test, much practice in parallel parking is essential.
6. Both the cover and the content should be considered when selecting a book as a gift.
7. Upset by the bad reviews, I vowed never to write another play.
8. Looking at the depressing list of available jobs, my decision to quit school seemed hasty.
9. By writing to the company, a person can receive a free catalogue.
10. To do this exercise, all aspects of grammar are essential.

C. Explain why the italicized modifiers were placed where they are rather than elsewhere in the sentence:

1. *"As we were thus engaged,* we saw a stag bound nimbly by, within about twenty paces of where we were sitting, and by its panting, it seemed prest by the hunters." (Oliver Goldsmith, *The Vicar of Wakefield*)
2. *"As soon as Mr. Bagshot had quitted the room,* the Count, *taking Wild by the hand,* told him he had something to communicate to him of very great importance." (Henry Fielding, *Jonathan Wild*)
3. "He went straight forward, *deviating at the church, where the crowd became thicker,* into the Rue du Faubourg Montmartre, and so to the boulevard, which he crossed." (Arnold Bennett, *The Old Wives' Tale*)
4. "Meanwhile the men stood in calm little groups, *chatting, smoking, pretending to pay no heed to the rustling animation of the women's world.*" (D. H. Lawrence, *Women in Love*)
5. *"Before I proceed to give an account of my leaving this Kingdom,* it may be proper to inform the Reader of a private Intrigue which had been for two Months forming against me." (Jonathan Swift, *Gulliver's Travels*)
6. *"From my boyish days* I had always felt a great perplexity on one point in *Macbeth.*" (Thomas De Quincey, "On the Knocking at the Gate in *Macbeth*")
7. *"On being teased by the reading and tweaked by the nurse,* the child will commonly begin to cry, which is reckoned a good sign, as showing a consciousness of guilt." (Samuel Butler, *Erewhon*)

8. "It was always a great affair, the Misses Morkan's annual dance. Everybody who knew them came to it, *members of the family, old friends of the family, the members of Julia's choir, any of Kate's pupils that were grown up enough, and even some of Mary Jane's pupils too.*" (James Joyce, "The Dead")

9. "A man's first care should be to avoid the reproaches of his own heart; his next, to escape the censures of the world. *If the last interferes with the former,* it ought to be entirely neglected." (Joseph Addison, *The Spectator,* No. 122)

10. "Tinglings of pleasure pervaded Car'line's spasmodic little frame *as she journeyed down with Ned to the place she had left two or three years before in silence and under a cloud.*" (Thomas Hardy, "The Fiddler of the Reels")

10

Compounding

A sentence consists of a subject and a predicate, the latter containing a verb and all required complements:

    10.1   The manager read a letter.

The verb may be expanded with auxiliaries:

    10.2   The manager *must have been reading* a letter.

Adverbials may be added to provide specific information about time, place, manner, and the like:

    10.3   The manager must have been reading a letter *during his coffee break*.

And noun phrases may contain determiners, adjectives, demonstratives, and other elements in addition to the noun:

    10.4   The *pudgy* manager must have been reading a *funny* letter during his *second* coffee break.

Even with these expansions, we still recognize the basic structure of
10.1.

We may also combine two sentences by subordinating one to the
other:

Relative Clause

10.5 We were talking to the people [who have just moved in
next door].

Noun Clause

10.6 They believe [that they are being watched].

Adverb Clause

10.7 He opened the package [although his father told him
not to].

Absolute Phrase

10.8 [The game being over], there was no point in our waiting longer.

Participial Phrase

10.9 [Combing the shag rug carefully], Doreen hunted for
her contact lens.

Gerund Phrase

10.10 Have you considered [asking Phil for a ride]?

Infinitive Phrase

10.11 I would hate [for you to get lost].

Although both embedded and main clauses are essential to the meaning, we do not give them equal importance. In most cases the main
clause expresses the principal idea, and the subordinate clause or
phrase gives one that is secondary.

COMPOUND SENTENCES

Instead of making one sentence subordinate to another, we can give them equal importance. Let us start with two separate sentences that are related in meaning:

> **10.12** Ethel opened the door with her key.

> **10.13** We then slipped into the laboratory.

If we found sentence **10.13** following **10.12** in a paragraph, we would assume that the act of opening the door preceded that of slipping into the laboratory, that the door was the one to the laboratory, and that Ethel's action made it possible for us to enter. Instead of writing these as two separate sentences, we could connect them more closely by joining them into one sentence punctuated with a semicolon:

> **10.14** Ethel opened the door with her key; we then slipped into the laboratory.

However, it is only on paper that **10.14** connects the ideas more closely than the succession **10.12** and **10.13** does. We would not hear a difference if the sentence were read aloud to us. To provide closer connection, we must add a word like *and:*

> **10.15** Ethel opened the door with her key, *and* we then slipped into the laboratory.

We still have two main clauses.

It is conventional to classify sentences according to the number and kinds of clauses they contain. A sentence consisting of only one main clause is known as a ***simple sentence:***

> **10.16** The attractive aborigine offered us a shrunken head.

Two or more main clauses joined together make up a ***compound sentence:***

> **10.17** The attractive aborigine offered us a shrunken head, but we did not buy it.

A combination of one main clause and one or more subordinate clauses is a ***complex sentence:***

> **10.18** Although the attractive aborigine offered us a shrunken head, we did not buy it.

And a combination of two or more main clauses and one or more subordinate clauses is known as a ***compound-complex sentence:***

160

10.19   Although the attractive aborigine offered us a shrunken head, we did not buy it; and we were sorry later.

Most compound sentences are derived from only two main clauses, but three or more are sometimes joined together:

10.20   I had nothing but bad luck yesterday. My television antenna blew down, my cat got hit by a car, someone stole my tape recorder, and I forgot my wife's birthday.

The first sentence provides the context. The second is a series of four simple sentences joined into one long compound sentence. It should be noted that we did not reach a limit with four connected sentences; we could have kept adding as long as we could think of misfortunes and as long as we held the attention of our listeners.

COORDINATING CONJUNCTIONS
AND CONJUNCTIVE ADVERBS

Words such as *and, but,* and *or* are known as **coordinating conjunctions** when they join two main clauses or other structures that are alike (e.g., two prepositional phrases, two adjectives, and so on). The choice of conjunctions determines how the clauses are related in meaning.

One relationship that clauses may share is called **additive;** that is, we intend *both:*

10.21a   Elizabeth will invite Cathy to the party, *and* she will invite Eloise.

At times we add other words to bring out this additive notion:

10.21b   Elizabeth will invite Cathy to the party, *and* she will invite Eloise *also.*

   c   Elizabeth will invite Cathy to the party, *and* she will invite Eloise *as well.*

   d   Elizabeth will invite Cathy to the party, *and* she will invite Eloise *too.*

Or with a slight change in structure we can use *both ... and:*

10.21e   Elizabeth will invite *both* Cathy *and* Eloise to the party.

The usual conjunction for the additive meaning is *and.*

At times *and* is used in a sense slightly different from that of the preceding sentences:

10.22 He hit me *and* hit me until my nose bled.

10.23 They stayed *and* stayed.

10.24 It got hotter *and* hotter that afternoon.

10.25 I tried *and* tried, but I still couldn't open the safe.

For some verbs such as *hit* this use of *and* means repetition; for others it indicates intensification.

A second relationship indicates a *choice* of one or the other:

10.26a Elizabeth will invite Cathy to the party, *or* she will invite Eloise.

At times *or* follows *either* to emphasize the notion of an alternative:

10.26b Elizabeth will invite *either* Cathy *or* Eloise to the party.

For negation we use *nor* or the combination *neither . . . nor:*

10.26c Elizabeth will not invite Cathy to the party, *nor* will she invite Eloise.

d Elizabeth will invite *neither* Cathy *nor* Eloise to the party.

Conjunctions that occur in pairs — *either . . . or, neither . . . nor, both . . . and,* and the like — are known as *correlatives.*

A third relationship expressed by coordinating conjunctions is *contrast:*

10.27 Elizabeth will invite Cathy to the party, *but* she won't invite Eloise.

10.28 I will do my best, *yet* that may not be enough.

Frequently one of the clauses is positive and the other negative, but other kinds of contrast are also possible:

10.29 The Pattersons are poor, but they send their daughter to an expensive private school.

10.30 He is an ichthyologist, but I enjoy talking to him.

10.31 Their daughter is over six feet tall, but she is friendly.

The contrast in **10.29** is between poverty and the ability to afford an expensive private school. That in **10.30** is less obvious, but it implies that the speaker normally does not enjoy talking to ichthyologists. Similarly, in **10.31** the speaker's opinion is that women over six feet tall are usually not friendly; this one is an exception. It should be obvious from these examples that the contrast does not have to reflect objective truth, but just the attitude of the speaker or writer.

The fourth relationship expressed by coordinating conjunctions is *reason:*

10.32a We knew that it would rain, *for* we could see the clouds overhead.

10.33a It began to rain, *so* we went inside.

These are easily paraphrased with adverb clauses with no loss in meaning:

10.32b We knew that it would rain [since we could see the clouds overhead].

10.33b [Since it began to rain], we went inside.

So is more common in conversation than in formal written English.

Closely related in meaning to certain coordinating conjunctions are the *conjunctive adverbs:*

10.34 We were comfortable enough in the room; *however,* we turned on the air conditioner anyway.

10.35 He couldn't hear what the speaker was saying; he, *therefore,* moved closer to the front.

10.36 I will not be finished with this novel by tomorrow; *moreover,* I probably won't be finished with it by next week.

Some other frequently used conjunctive adverbs are *consequently, nevertheless, hence, otherwise, conversely,* and *still.*

Although coordinating conjunctions and conjunctive adverbs have some similarities in meaning, they differ in where they may occur. Coordinating conjunctions always come at the beginning of the clause:

10.37a He was tall, *but* he couldn't reach the ceiling.

b *He was tall, he *but* couldn't reach the ceiling.

c *He was tall, he couldn't reach the ceiling *but.*

This initial position also holds true for the beginning of a sentence when an idea is carried over from a preceding one:

10.38 *And* they never discovered the source of the odor.

Conjunctive adverbs may occur at the beginning of the sentence, but they also come in other positions as well:

10.39a *Therefore,* we stopped eating in that cafeteria.

b We, *therefore,* stopped eating in that cafeteria.

10.40a He resigned as treasurer; *however,* he did remain a member of the club.

b He resigned as treasurer; he did, *however,* remain a member of the club.

c He resigned as treasurer; he did remain a member of the club, *however.*

Conjunctive adverbs function like parenthetical expressions such as *on the other hand* and *as a matter of fact.*

PUNCTUATION OF COMPOUND SENTENCES

A comma usually precedes a coordinating conjunction that joins two independent clauses:

10.41 He gave a long-winded account of how he was almost late getting to the theater, and then he told us that the rehearsal had been called off.

10.42 He could hear us very well, but he didn't answer.

When *and* joins two short independent clauses, the comma is frequently omitted:

10.43 Hal saw his mistake and he turned red.

As with introductory modifiers, there is no clear-cut line between "short" and "long" independent clauses, and practices of punctuation by educated writers vary.

When two independent clauses are not joined with a coordinating conjunction, they are punctuated as separate sentences or as one sentence with a semicolon:

10.44a Snow has been on the ground for over a month, and the sun has appeared only sporadically.

b Snow has been on the ground for over a month; the sun has appeared only sporadically.

c Snow has been on the ground for over a month. The sun has appeared only sporadically.

The difference between using a semicolon and separating the two clauses into individual sentences depends upon how closely related the ideas are.

Like other parenthetical expressions, conjunctive adverbs are set off with commas:

10.45a *Nevertheless,* we were eager to hear the results.

b We were, *nevertheless,* eager to hear the results.

Some authors regularly place a comma before *and* in a series; others omit it.

When appositives consist of a series of conjoined noun phrases, they are usually set off with dashes or colons:

10.60   Everyone in the room — the Smiths, Dr. Collins, and the Dean — could hear what you said.

10.61   Leyden, Göttingen, and Cambridge — these are the universities he visited while in Europe.

10.62   She is taking the following courses: Shakespeare, Italian Composition, Advanced Calculus, Harmony, and Art Appreciation.

The colon is used only when the series ends the sentence. Also, special punctuation is needed when the items within a series contain internal commas:

10.63   They rejected Paul, Rachel's nephew; my cousin; Robert, my cousin's friend; and several others.

The items are separated from one another with a semicolon for clarity.

PARALLEL STRUCTURE

We may join two or more like structures, such as prepositional phrases:

10.64   We looked under the rug and in the closet.

Both *under the rug* and *in the closet* function as adverbials of place. If we try joining an adverbial of place with one of time, we produce an unacceptable sentence:

10.65   *We looked under the rug and at noon.

The conjunction of two unlike structures such as an adverbial of time and one of place is known as *faulty parallelism.*

Here are some other examples of conjoined structures that are not parallel; the **b** versions provide suggested revisions in which the same kinds of structures are joined:

10.66a   He is strong but a fool. (*But* joins an adjective and a noun phrase.)

   b   He is strong but foolish. (*But* joins two adjectives.)

10.67a   So that she could save money and to avoid eating with unpleasant people, Connie claimed that she had a previous engagement. (*And* joins an adverb clause and an infinitive phrase.)

b   To save money and to avoid eating with unpleasant people, Connie claimed that she had a previous engagement. (*And* joins two infinitive phrases.)

The longer the structures are, the more likely we are to join two that are not parallel. In speaking, we do not always plan a sentence before we start it, but rather think of new directions as we are talking. As a result, we frequently join unlike structures. In writing, where there is opportunity for revision, we try to avoid faulty parallelism.

THE ORDER OF CONJOINED ELEMENTS

Although compound constructions are traditionally said to be of equal importance, there is sometimes a notion of priority implied by the order in which they appear. Whether we address two people as *Malcolm and Norma* or as *Norma and Malcolm* may imply a degree of preference. Also, the ordering may be one of convention, such as *Mom and Dad* rather than *Dad and Mom* or *ladies and gentlemen* instead of *gentlemen and ladies.*

The ordering of some structures suggests a time sequence and a cause-and-effect relationship:

10.68   Bill saw the smoke and opened the door.

10.69   Bill opened the door and saw the smoke.

In **10.68** we assume that Bill saw the smoke before he opened the door; in **10.69** we accept the opposite sequence. We also assume that the earlier event prompted the latter.

However, when we join two structures that describe events that could not have affected each other, neither time sequence nor cause and effect is assumed:

10.70   Her mother was born in Canada, and her father was born in Peru.

10.71   Her father was born in Peru, and her mother was born in Canada.

We do not think that either birth was the cause of the other, nor do we make any assumptions about whether the father or the mother is the older. In sentences such as these, the conventional notion of equal importance for compound structures holds.

COMPOUNDING AND SUBJECT-VERB AGREEMENT

For most speakers of English, verbs agree with their subjects in a fairly consistent manner. For verbs other than *be,* the present tense has an *-s* ending for third-person singular: *he writes, she sleeps, the cactus seems.* For first and second persons there is no such ending: *I write, sleep, seem; you write, sleep, seem.* Nor is there an ending for the plural. A sample conjugation will illustrate:

I write	we write
you write	you write
he writes	they write

In the past tense there is no differentiation, regardless of person or number:

I wrote	we wrote
you wrote	you wrote
he wrote	they wrote

For the verb *be* there are additional distinctions, both for the present and past tenses:

I am	we are
you are	you are
he is	they are

I was	we were
you were	you were
he was	they were

For most people these conventions follow regularly whenever the subject is clear.

However, whenever the structure of the sentence becomes so complicated that the subject is not immediately apparent, many people hesitate over problems of subject-verb agreement; that is, for an easy sentence such as the following, only the a version is likely to occur:

10.72a Some snakes are in the yard.

   b *Some snakes is in the yard.

Yet when the subject is placed after the verb, as in a sentence beginning with *there,* it is no longer so obviously the subject:

10.72c   There are some snakes in the yard.

This fuzziness is increased with compound noun phrases functioning as subject:

10.73a   A motorcycle, a car, and a bicycle were in the garage.

   b   There were a motorcycle, a car, and a bicycle in the garage.

Whereas most people would not say,

10.74 *They was in the garage.

the compound noun phrase creates enough confusion over the sentence structure that they may hesitate over whether to use *was* or *were* in **10.73,** both **a** and **b.** Once the sentence structure is clarified, the problem of the choice of verbs vanishes. Even still, compound structures with *there* are frequently seen with singular verbs even in edited works:

10.75   There was no enthusiasm shown during the class and no sadness when it was over.

10.76   There is a time to make love and a time to fight.

This preference for singular subjects is no doubt a result of two factors: the length of the elements of the compound, of which the first is singular; and the use of *a, no,* or other indefinites such as *every, each,* and the like.

We normally find singular verbs with certain conjoined subjects like the following:

10.77   First her son and then her daughter was in the hospital.

10.78   Each girl and each boy was congratulated.

10.79   Every flower and every bush is to be cut down.

Also, when the conjoined noun phrases form a unit, they are treated as singular:

10.80   My friend and advisor has agreed to lend me his car.

10.81   Macaroni and cheese is not good when it is cold.

We see not only the singular verbs *has* and *is,* but also singular pronouns (*his* and *it*) referring to the combination. At times abstract nouns may be thought of as forming a unit:

10.82   Charles' love and affection for his wife was so intense that he did not suspect her of infidelity.

Some people might argue that *love* and *affection* mean the same thing; one should be omitted to avoid redundancy. Others see a shade of difference and feel that the inclusion of both words is appropriate. Although many rule books say to treat compounds such as *love and affection* as plurals, actual practice in printed works varies.

Finally, when subjects differing in number are joined by *either ... or* or *neither ... nor,* most rule books say that we should make the verb agree with the closer subject:

> **10.83**   Neither her mother nor her friends were there.

> **10.84**   Neither her friends nor her mother was there.

Many people avoid structures like this by recasting the sentence:

> **10.85**   Her mother was not there, nor were her friends.

Similarly, when the first-person pronoun *I* is the closer subject in such a compound, the verb theoretically agrees with it:

> **10.86**   Neither the Daltons nor I am to blame.

This can be recast as follows:

> **10.87**   The Daltons are not to blame; neither am I.

Many people avoid structures that attract attention, even though rule books may sanction them.

EXERCISES

A. Locate the coordinating conjunctions and name the structures that they join (infinitive phrases, noun clauses, etc.):

1. Rachel did not answer any of the letters that her mother wrote her, and she even refused to read some of them.
2. She answered all the questions rapidly but accurately.
3. The old man left his children and his widow only a small portion of his estate.
4. He was embarrassed to remain in the room after confessing his misdemeanor, so he tried to slip out the door without being noticed.
5. The student whom everyone praised and who looked very promising became a recluse before she was thirty.
6. It is amusing to have everyone think you are knowledgeable but in reality not know what anyone is talking about.

7. Will you be here Monday or Wednesday?
8. Taking aspirin, resting in bed, and drinking liquids will help you get rid of your cold.
9. Your fingernails are clean, but your neck isn't.
10. Why did you watch me make that gaffe but say nothing about it?

B. Revise the following sentences to correct the faulty parallelism:

1. Martin being always in a hurry, but he never got to work on time.
2. They are people whom we not only can't stand but who insist upon having us to dinner at least once a week.
3. They vacationed in Switzerland, ate fondue, photographed Mont Blanc, the Matterhorn, the Jungfrau, went mountain climbing, skiing, skating, and hated to come home.
4. She was a good conversationalist, a fine movie critic, and served splendidly as president of the organization.
5. Ruby was quick to forget trivial insults, slow to lose her temper, and everyone respected her.
6. Thomas is not only stupid, but he is sarcastic.
7. Eunice works eight hours a day, does her own cooking, and takes care of her invalid aunt, but which does not prevent her from attending every meeting of the Serpentine Club.
8. I like to walk in the rain because of its refreshing nature and because it cools me off.
9. Although he was more intelligent than anyone else in his class, he never made fun of others for their mistakes but constantly trying to improve his own understanding of calculus.
10. He is the kind of professor always seen in hotel lobbies at conventions but who never goes to hear any papers read.

C. At times the ordering of conjoined structures can be altered without serious consequences, but at others a difference in meaning results. Comment on the ordering of the conjoined structures in the following sentences:

1. "I came; I saw; I conquered." (Caesar)
2. Would you rather go to a movie or stay home?
3. Would you like to stay home and watch television?
4. "In the spring a fuller crimson comes upon the robin's breast;
   In the spring the wanton lapwing gets himself another crest;
   In the spring a livelier iris changes on the burnished dove;

> In the spring a young man's fancy lightly turns to thoughts of
>   love." (Tennyson)
5. "It is an ancient Mariner
>   And he stoppeth one of three." (Coleridge)
6. "When shall we three meet again
>   In thunder, lightning or in rain?" (Shakespeare)
7. "To Mercy, Pity, Peace, and Love,
>   All pray in their distress." (Blake)
8. "I look into my glass.
>   And view my wasting skin,
>   And say, 'Would God it came to pass
>   My heart had shrunk as thin!'" (Hardy)
9. "Stone walls do not a prison make,
>   Nor iron bars a cage." (Lovelace)
10. "It was the best of times, it was the worst of times, it was the
>   age of wisdom, it was the age of foolishness, it was the epoch
>   of belief, it was the epoch of incredulity, it was the season of
>   Light, it was the season of Darkness, it was the spring of hope,
>   it was the winter of despair, we had everything before us, we
>   had nothing before us, we were all going direct to Heaven,
>   we were all going direct the other way—in short, the period
>   was so far like the present period, that some of its noisiest
>   authorities insisted on its being received, for good or for evil,
>   in the superlative degree of comparison only." (Dickens)

D. Supply commas, colons, semicolons, and dashes as needed according to the rules for standard English:

1. At the beginning he could barely stand to listen to the sym-
   phony but after the first movement he found it to be quite
   enjoyable.
2. His three daughters Eleanor Rosie and Penelope all answered
   the announcement in the newspaper.
3. Henry's older brother stood in the pouring rain a healthy vigor-
   ous man in his early twenties.
4. When he discovered that he had left his coat in his seat at the
   movie theater he was already half way home.
5. Two officials namely the secretary and the treasurer have given
   their resignations to the president who reluctantly accepted
   them.
6. I have never enjoyed reading Edna Ferber's novels however I
   do like the movie versions of them.

7. In the middle of the street in front of our house there was a broken gas main so we had to leave the neighborhood until the gas company could repair it.

8. She wore her old yellow hat which she had been saving for such an occasion.

9. To reach my lake cottage you should go south on highway forty and exit at the intersection with Colton Avenue.

10. He sometimes reads the *Clarion* a small-town weekly newspaper that prints mostly lurid gossipy columns.

11. Her son Thomas is more trustworthy than any of her other children living at home.

12. A real daughter of her time Abigail refused to marry any man whose lips had touched liquor.

13. She had never taken a singing lesson in her life nevertheless she assaulted our nerves with her rendition of "Silent Night."

14. All I could understand were the words *apathy* and *heart* neither of which made much sense to me.

15. We were studying the play *Macbeth* Shakespeare's shortest tragedy.

16. I added the word *toothsome* which seemed to make the passage more interesting.

17. I was pleased to find the poem "To a Mouse" in the anthology even though my favorite poem "The Cotter's Saturday Night" was not included.

18. Upset by his daughter's choice of a husband Mr. Cramer was courteous and did not make a scene even though he felt like hitting the numbskull she had chosen.

19. My mother's youngest brother a conscientious scholarly gentleman advised his only son Edward to become a tramp but he decided to become a professional window washer.

20. Excited by the publicity the Helen Dawes who received all the attention didn't explain the error that had been made.

21. I feel more comfortable with the devil that I know than with the one which I haven't even met yet.

22. Your brother Frank has all the traits that I despise most pomposity aggressiveness and self-righteousness.

23. Those four cars the Chevrolet the Ford the Dodge and the Mercury will have to be moved.

24. The following students received special recognition Louise Johnson who hadn't opened a book all semester Tony Appleton who hadn't been to more than half the class meetings and Cora Snodgrass who had cheated on every exam.

25. We could not continue to exist without the sun which is our source of light.
26. I visited my brother Martin who lives in Los Angeles but he was too busy to show me the sights.
27. The way she answered made me think of my sister Anna.
28. Those who do not work or attend class regularly will probably fail the course those who come to every class meeting however will not necessarily receive good grades.

11

Pronouns

Instead of referring to people or things with full noun phrases, we frequently use pronouns, especially when we do not know their identity:

11.1 *Who* unlocked the desk?

11.2 *What* did you find in the closet?

11.3 *Someone* knocked on the door but left before I could answer it.

11.4 *Something* must be wrong.

Beyond knowing whether the noun phrases name humans or not, we have no information about them.

A second reason for using pronouns is to avoid repetition. Once we mention people, we usually do not continue referring to them with their names:

11.5a **Jim* went to the library at eight o'clock, and *Jim* stayed until closing time.

11.6a *The woman* waited in the hall, but *the woman* wouldn't give us *the woman's* name.

In each sentence we replace all but one of these noun phrases with pronouns:

11.5b *Jim* went to the library at eight o'clock, and *he* stayed until closing time.

11.6b *The woman* waited in the hall, but *she* wouldn't give us *her* name.

This chapter will be concerned with the uses of pronouns.

PRONOUNS AND THEIR ANTECEDENTS

In earlier chapters we saw that pronouns replace entire noun phrases, not just nouns:

11.7a *The young woman on the corner waved when we looked at the young woman on the corner.

b *The young woman on the corner waved when we looked at the young *her* on the corner.

c The young woman on the corner waved when we looked at *her*.

If we use a pronoun, it must stand for the entire noun phrase *the young woman on the corner,* not just the noun *woman.* The fact that some noun phrases consist of a single word makes it seem that pronouns at times replace just nouns rather than entire noun phrases:

11.8a *Herbert* likes *spinach.*

b *He* likes *it.*

However, it should be remembered that *Herbert* and *spinach* are noun phrases as well as nouns.

We speak of the noun phrase that means the same thing as a pronoun as its **antecedent;** hence, in **11.7c** we say that the antecedent of *her* is *the young woman on the corner* or just *woman.* Since the prefix *ante-* means "before," the usual place for the antecedent is before the pronoun; however, there are some exceptions, as we shall see presently.

In compound sentences pronouns never occur before their antecedents:

11.9a *He* is usually rude to uninvited guests, but *Paul* looked glad to see us last night.

    b *Paul* is usually rude to uninvited guests, but *he* looked glad to see us last night.

If *he* and *Paul* are the same person, sentence **11.9a** is not possible.

When a sentence contains a dependent clause or a phrase, it is sometimes possible for the pronoun to precede its antecedent:

    11.10a The speaker was ridiculing functional illiterates, even though he could barely read himself.

    b *He was ridiculing functional illiterates, even though the speaker could barely read himself.

    c Even though the speaker could barely read himself, he was ridiculing functional illiterates.

    d Even though he could barely read himself, the speaker was ridiculing functional illiterates.

We may pronominalize the first noun phrase when it is in a dependent construction, such as **11.10d;** otherwise, as we can see from **11.10b,** the antecedent must precede the pronoun.

In gerund, infinitive, and participial phrases, we frequently find pronouns, regardless of where the phrase occurs:

    11.11a Judy, trying to look *her* best for the interview, took out her gum.

    b Trying to look *her* best for the interview, Judy took out her gum.

    c Judy took out her gum, trying to look *her* best for the interview.

    11.12a To make people like *him* better, Charles began telling jokes.

    b Charles began telling jokes to make people like *him* better.

We can say that these sentences follow the same principles as those with dependent clauses, such as **11.10d,** or we can say that the real antecedent in each sentence is not *Judy* in **11.11** or *Charles* in **11.12,** but the understood subject of the participial or infinitive phrase.

When a sentence contains more than one noun, there is usually no confusion over which one is the antecedent:

    11.13 Perry thanked the twins for the invitation, but *he* could not go to the party.

    11.14 Randy thanked Ellen for the present, but *he* gave *her* nothing in return.

11.15 Perry thanked Randy for the invitation, but *he* could not accept *it*.

In **11.13,** *the twins* cannot be the antecedent for *he* because it is plural; *Perry, the invitation,* and *the party* are the only other noun phrases in the sentence, and *the invitation* and *the party* are nonhuman, requiring *it*. In **11.14,** as there are two human nouns that differ in sex, we know that *he* refers to *Randy, her* to *Ellen*. In **11.15,** *it* clearly refers to *the invitation,* the only nonhuman noun in the sentence. Although *he* could potentially refer to either masculine noun, the context shows that it means *Perry,* not *Randy*.

There are other sentences, however, in which confusion is possible:

11.16a Beth told Sandra that *she* would be late.

Both nouns are feminine, and the context does not rule out either one. We do not permit the repetition of the proper noun even for the purpose of clarity:

11.16b *Beth told Sandra that Beth would be late.

c *Beth told Sandra that Sandra would be late.

Some people write the antecedent in parentheses after the pronoun:

11.16d Beth told Sandra that she (Beth) would be late.

e Beth told Sandra that she (Sandra) would be late.

William Faulkner used this device at times, but for less experienced writers it is clumsy. Most people recast the sentence in a way that makes the reference clear:

11.16f Beth told Sandra, "I will be late."

g Beth told Sandra, "You will be late."

Unfortunately, there is no single solution that works for all kinds of sentences.

As we have seen in the preceding examples, pronouns agree with their antecedents in gender; that is, *she* refers to women, girls, and certain female animals. We also use *she* for a few inanimate objects such as ships, countries, and cars of which we are fond. *He* is used for men, boys, and some male animals. *It* refers to inanimate objects and to most animals. People vary in the pronouns they use for cats, dogs, horses, and cows. Some use *he* or *she* when they know the sex of the animal, especially if they call it by name, such as *Ginger* or *Ishmael*. Others use *it* for all animals. For most birds, reptiles, fish, and animals, the usual pronoun is *it,* even when we know the sex. On rare occasions we may use *it* when referring to a human, such as a baby when the speaker does not know the sex. Most mothers are not offended by "What's its name?" but they may be if they are inappropriately asked "What's her name?" or "What's his name?" Also, parents often refer to babies before birth as *it* unless they are hoping for a child of a given sex or medical tests have predicted whether it will be a girl or a boy.

When we refer to humans of either sex (e.g., *a person, anyone, a teacher*), there is no satisfactory neutral pronoun in English. For many years, *he* was considered the appropriate choice:

> **11.17a**   If anyone calls while I'm out, ask *him* to call back later.

Although this practice was followed in most kinds of writing, many people did not feel comfortable with it in speech. *Him* in **11.17a** did not seem really neutral, but rather an assumption that the caller would be a male. The plural *them* was often used since it did not indicate sex:

> **11.17b**   If anyone calls while I'm out, ask *them* to call back later.

English teachers gritted their teeth over this illogical use of the plural *them* to refer to one person (*anyone*). They also winced over the use of the wordy *him or her:*

> **11.17c**   If anyone calls while I'm out, ask *him or her* to call back later.

Today many people accept the previously taboo structures of **11.17b** and **11.17c**. We also find others continuing to use *he* when the sex is not specified. Still others avoid the problem by recasting the sentence in the plural. Here are the possibilities:

> **11.18a**   When a person goes to the grocery store, he often finds that prices have risen.
>
> **b**   When a person goes to the grocery store, they often find that prices have risen.
>
> **c**   When a person goes to the grocery store, he or she often finds that prices have risen.
>
> **d**   When a person goes to the grocery store, (s)he often finds that prices have risen.
>
> **e**   When people go to the grocery store, they often find that prices have risen.
>
> **f**   When we go to the grocery store, we often find that prices have risen.

The last two versions avoid the problems of referring to a woman as *he* (**11.18a**), using the plural *they* for a singular (**11.18b**), being wordy

(**11.18c**), and being overly clever (**11.18d**). However, the final choice has to rest with the individual.

The acceptance of previously taboo phrases such as *he or she* provides a good example of the origin of standards. Dictionaries and other reference works base their rules on the actual usage of educated people; they do not legislate. During the period that *he or she* was gaining widespread acceptance, most rule books still recorded the older standard. Once structures such as this become accepted, reference works change their statements.

At times writers of rule books tried to formulate their rules according to what seemed logical to them rather than what educated people were using. We find, for example, the statement that if the antecedent of a pronoun is a compound joined by *or,* the pronoun agrees in gender with the closer one:

> **11.19**   Rupert or Caroline will bring *her* book.
> **11.20**   Caroline or Rupert will bring *his* book.

Similarly, if the members of the compound antecedent differ in number, the pronoun agrees with the closer:

> **11.21**   The teacher or the students will give *their* view.
> **11.22**   The students or the teacher will give *his* view.

In actual practice, few writers would use sentences such as these. Instead, they revise them:

> **11.23**   Rupert will bring his book, or Caroline will bring hers.
> **11.24**   Either the teacher will give his view, or the students will give theirs.

Legislative bodies may devise rules for driving cars on city streets, building houses, and smoking in public places. Most people will then follow them even if they have never done so in the past or even if the rules are illogical. Language is different in that it existed long before any rules were written down.

INTENSIVE AND REFLEXIVE PRONOUNS

English has a set of pronouns ending in *-self* that are not usually interchangeable with other pronouns:

myself	ourselves
yourself	yourselves
himself, herself, itself, oneself	themselves

Most of these are formed by adding *-self* or the plural *-selves* to the possessive: *my* + *self, your* + *selves,* and the like. Two are irregular. Instead of the expected *hisself* and *theirselves,* we find forms based on the objectives *him* and *them: himself, themselves.* Those speakers of English who use *hisself* and *theirselves* have regularized the forms. This is another example of standard usage being determined by the practices of educated speakers and writers, not by logic.

These pronouns are said to be ***intensive*** when they are used as appositives to emphasize another noun or pronoun:

   11.25a   William *himself* opened the safe.

   b   William opened the safe *himself.*

   11.26a   Cora *herself* will preside over the ceremony.

   b   Cora will preside over the ceremony *herself.*

Intensive pronouns agree with their antecedents; we could not use *herself, ourselves, themselves,* or any pronoun other than *himself* in **11.25.** Nor could we use any pronoun other than *herself* in **11.26.** In imperatives the intensive pronoun agrees with the understood subject *you:*

   11.27   Do it *yourself.*

Again, no other pronoun is possible, unless we shift to the plural *yourselves.*

Intensive pronouns may be used with nouns and pronouns that function as objects, appositives, and predicate nouns as well as subjects:

   11.28   We thanked the queen *herself.*

   11.29   We should send it to the employees *themselves.*

   11.30   That was the doctor *herself* speaking.

   11.31   Let's do it *ourselves.*

In their ability to accompany nouns in any function, intensive pronouns are like other appositives.

Pronouns ending in *-self* may also be used as ***reflexives.*** In this function they are usually direct objects, but they may be objects of prepositions or predicate pronouns:

   11.32   I kicked *myself.* (direct object)

   11.33   Tom and Lillie baked the pie for *themselves.* (object of a preposition)

   11.34   She hasn't been *herself* lately. (predicate pronoun)

Also, the antecedent of a reflexive is normally a subject, but occasionally it may serve some other function:

11.35   I gave Henry the tie for *himself*.

In **11.35**, the antecedent is an indirect object.

When two noun phrases within a clause refer to the same person or thing, the second must be a reflexive unless it is a possessive:

11.36a   *Terry likes Terry too much.

    b   *Terry likes him too much.

    c   Terry likes himself too much.

    d   *Himself likes Terry too much.

11.37   Terry likes his toys too much.

Sentence **11.36a** shows that we cannot use the full noun both times, and the **b** version shows that the simple pronoun *him* is not possible if it means the same person as *Terry*. The **d** version shows that the reflexive must follow its antecedent, not precede it. Only the **c** version with the reflexive *himself* or **11.37** with the possessive *his* is possible.

These observations are also true for embedded sentences:

11.38a   I said that John cut me.

    b   *I said that John cut myself.

11.39a   He said that John cut him.

    b   He said that John cut himself.

Although the antecedent for *me/myself* is in the same overall sentence (**11.38**) as the pronoun, it is not in the same clause; hence, only *me* is possible. In **11.39**, if *John* and *him/himself* are the same person, only *himself* may be used. In **11.39a**, we understand *him* to mean *he* or someone else, not *John*.

When a pronoun in a gerund, infinitive, or participial phrase refers to the same person or thing as the understood subject of the phrase, the pronoun is a reflexive:

11.40   Garland wanted [to serve *himself*].

11.41   [To make *herself* appear taller], Sally stood on the top step.

11.42   The woman [helping *herself* to the oranges] hasn't found the rotten ones yet.

11.43   [Looking at *herself* in the mirror], Frances frowned.

11.44   Their worst fault is [fooling *themselves*].

11.45   [Belittling *ourselves*] is not something we often do.

11.46   [Helping *oneself*] is customary in this store.

11.47   It's no crime [to defend *yourself*].

If we did not take into account the understood subjects of these phrases, there would appear to be no system for using reflexive pronouns. In **11.41, 11.43,** and **11.45** the reflexive precedes the noun that appears to be its antecedent, yet we saw earlier that this order is normally not possible. Sentences **11.46** and **11.47** do not even have antecedents for the reflexives. Furthermore, in **11.40–11.45** what appears to be the antecedent is not in the same phrase as the pronoun. When we realize that the actual antecedents of these reflexives are the understood subjects of their phrases, everything becomes perfectly regular. Reflexives follow their antecedents, and both are in the same phrase. Even in **11.46** if we think of *helping oneself* as a reduction of *one's helping oneself,* the pronoun does have an antecedent, although understood. Similarly, in **11.47** we understand *to defend yourself* to mean *for you to defend yourself.*

These uses of reflexive pronouns have been in existence for many centuries, and virtually all speakers and writers use them in the same way, whether they are Englishmen, Scots, New Zealanders, Canadians, Bostonians, or Texans; whether they are writing a formal paper or a note on a Christmas card; whether they are arguing a case before the Supreme Court or chatting about the weather with a member of the family.

There are times, however, in which we find the reflexive *myself* where we would normally expect *I* or *me:*

11.48   "He would needs carry Will Wimble and myself with him to the county assizes." [Joseph Addison, *The Spectator,* No. 122]

11.49   The guests were received by Mrs. Martin and myself.

11.50   No one but the manager and myself knew what was going on.

These uses of *myself* without an antecedent normally occur in compounds, although they can occasionally be found by themselves in complex sentences:

11.51   Although he would have preferred to complain to someone in authority, there was no one around for him to speak to but myself.

The fact that these antecedentless reflexives occur primarily in compounds suggests that they are the result of the speaker's confusion over their function in the sentence. This assumption is strengthened when we hear people changing constructions, such as a guide for a tour of an American city who wanted the people to know that when they came out of the museum the bus would be parked in a different place from where they left it. Either he or the driver would be available to direct them to the bus. To make sure that everyone understood, he repeated his information five or six times. He first said:

11.52a   When you come out of the museum, look for the driver or me.

This was changed the second time to:

11.52b   When you come out of the museum, look for the driver or I.

Finally, he changed to the reflexive:

11.52c   When you come out of the museum, look for the driver or myself.

He settled on this form for the remaining repetitions. Such antecedent-less reflexives are found fairly often in informal speech, but only rarely in print other than in conversation from novels or short stories. However, the sentence from Addison (11.48) was included to show that this use of the reflexive is not confined to the uneducated, nor is it an innovation of the twentieth century.

PRONOUN CASE FORMS

Except for possessives, nouns in English do not change according to their use in the sentence. Whether *the electrician* is a subject, a direct object, an appositive, or a predicate noun, it appears in the same form. Most pronouns, however, have two forms other than the possessive. Sometimes these are called *nominative* and *accusative,* the terms used for two cases in such classical languages as Latin, Greek, Gothic, and Sanskrit. Because the accusative in these languages is used for only some of the functions of the English objective, we are not using this term. Instead, we shall refer to the pronoun forms as **nominative, objective,** and **possessive.** We can list them as follows:

Nominative	Objective	Possessive
I	me	my, mine
you	you	your, yours
he	him	his
she	her	her, hers
it	it	its

we	us	our, ours
they	them	their, theirs
who	whom	whose

The other pronouns in English do not change in form other than for the possessive (*anyone, anyone's,* etc.).

Except for *his, its,* and *whose,* there are two possessive forms for each pronoun. We use *my, your, her, our,* and *their* when a noun follows; we use *mine, yours, hers, ours,* and *theirs* when the noun has been deleted:

11.53a   This is *my* book.

   b   This is *mine.*

11.54a   *Your* coat is on the floor.

   b   *Yours* is on the floor.

11.55a   We cleaned *her* car inside and out.

   b   We cleaned *hers* inside and out.

11.56a   *Their* house is older than *our* house.

   b   *Theirs* is older than *ours.*

Instead of *hers, his, theirs, yours,* and *ours,* some people use the non-standard *hern, hisn, theirn, yourn,* and *ourn,* forms patterned after *mine.* For standard written English only the forms ending in *-s* are used.

In simple sentences there is no variation among speakers in their use of nominative and objective pronouns:

11.57a   *We* do not agree.

   b   **Us* do not agree.

11.58a   We saw *them.*

   b   **We saw *they.*

11.59a   He gave *her* the money.

   b   **He gave *she* the money.

11.60a   We rode with *him.*

   b   **We rode with *he.*

Since *you* and *it* have the same forms for both cases, we have not illustrated them. For sentences such as 11.57–11.60, everyone uses the nominative for subjects and the objective for the various objects, regardless of how formal or informal the occasion may be or the speaker's regional and social background.

When these pronouns are parts of compound noun phrases, however, not everyone uses the same forms. Let us start with the system found in most grammars as the usage of formal written English and that of most educated speakers. According to this system, compounds are treated the same as single pronouns:

Subject

11.61a *Harold and she* will host the next meeting.

    b *She* will host the next meeting.

Direct Object

11.62a Everyone in the office thanked *Laura and me* for our conscientious work.

    b Everyone in the office thanked *me* for our conscientious work.

Indirect Object

11.63a You have sent *the accountant and us* the wrong forms.

    b You have sent *us* the wrong forms.

Object of a Preposition

11.64a The project was at last completed by *the contractor and him.*

    b The project was at last completed by *him.*

When the pronoun is an appositive, it is in the same case as the noun it renames:

Appositive to a Subject

11.65 Everyone in the hall — *Terry, Claudia, and she* — could hear what you were saying.

Appositive to a Direct Object

11.66 He could see both climbers: *Allen and him.*

Appositve to an Object of a Preposition

11.67 He will mail the brochure to everyone on the list: *the thirty members, the chairman, and her.*

Appositives following *let's* or *let us* are in the objective case, agreeing with *us:*

    11.68   Let's *you and me* climb this tree.

T. S. Eliot, of course, used *I* in the opening line of "The Love Song of J. Alfred Prufrock":

    11.69   "Let us go, then, you and I,"

Eliot notwithstanding, these forms are the ones normally found in books, magazines, newspapers, and journals issued by reputable publishing houses. To make compounds clearer, people are often told to recast them with single pronouns, such as the **b** versions of **11.61–11.64.**

Among speakers of English there is often a great deal of nervousness over being "right." They feel comfortable with choosing pronouns for simple sentences such as **11.57–11.60;** but when they have to use sentences in which the structure is not clear, such as compounds, they are less confident. Some decide that their natural inclination is normally wrong, and they go in the opposite direction; others settle upon nominatives for all compounds as the genteel choice. Hence, we hear sentences such as these:

    11.70   Between you and I, he'll never make it.

    11.71   He gave it to Fred and he.

    11.72   Did you see Rita and she?

Thomas Pyles in *The Origins and Development of the English Language* cites two such examples spoken by Queen Elizabeth II and President Dwight D. Eisenhower, respectively:

    11.73   "It is a wonderful moment for my husband and I after nearly six months away to be met and escorted by ships of the Home Fleet."

    11.74   "I am deeply honored that so many of you should have come down to welcome Mrs. Eisenhower and I back to Washington."

Nominative forms for all compounds were at one time heard only among the semieducated. They are now found frequently in the conversation of characters in comic strips, novels, short stories, plays, and television programs. They are even heard occasionally at scholarly conventions and in English Department faculty meetings. As sentences **11.73** and **11.74** show, they may be present in the speech of British monarchs and American presidents.

Compounding is not the only process that obscures the structure of a sentence and makes the choice of pronouns confusing. Pronouns followed by appositives may be equally troublesome:

11.75a   *We* committee members are overworked.

11.76a   They gave it to *us* convicts.

In **11.75a,** *we* is the subject and *committee members* is an appositive. In **11.76a,** *us* is the object of the preposition *to,* and it takes the appositive *convicts.* The structure is clearer if the appositive is left out:

11.75b   *We* are overworked.

11.76b   They gave it to *us.*

A third cause for obscure sentence structure is the deletion of part of a clause:

11.77a   We are taller than *she.*

11.78a   Did he pay you as much as *me?*

Apparently some people tend to think of *than* and *as* as prepositions rather than subordinate conjunctions. We may expand the dependent clauses so that all understood material is included:

11.77b   We are taller than *she is.*

11.78b   Did he pay you as much as *he paid me?*

The functions of the pronouns are much clearer when understood material is provided.

Interruption of normal word order is the fourth cause for confusion over sentence structure that results in hesitation over pronoun forms. Speakers of English are so accustomed to the SVO order that they tend to equate position before the verb with the nominative case and position after it with the objective; in addition, they recognize the position immediately following a preposition as that of the objective. Because questions move a pronoun to the beginning of the sentence, the normal word order is disrupted unless this pronoun is the subject. Relying on the position of the pronoun in relation to the verb rather than on its function, many people use *who* in all instances, as in the **b** versions of the following sentences. The forms preferred in formal written English are given in the **a** sentences.

11.79a   Who is going with you?

   b   Who is going with you?

11.80a   Whom did they send?

b   Who did they send?

11.81a Whom did you leave it with?

b   Who did you leave it with?

However, if the preposition immediately precedes the pronoun, everyone feels comfortable with *whom:*

11.81c With whom did you leave it?

This pattern of nominative pronouns before the verb, objectives after it and after prepositions can also be seen in the **b** versions of the following sentences with relative and noun clauses:

11.82a I gave it to the man whom you indicated.

b   I gave it to the man who you indicated.

11.83a Did you know whom he wanted?

b   Did you know who he wanted?

Relative pronouns functioning as objects are often deleted in sentences such as **11.82;** there is, therefore, no problem in choosing between *who* and *whom* when there is no pronoun.

To those people who are insecure about their use of pronouns, the inverted word order of questions, relative clauses, and noun clauses obscures the functions of the pronouns. Either rejecting the form that seems natural or opting for *whom* as the more elegant, they sometimes hit on the form used in standard English; at other times they overcorrect their usage, using *whom* where standard English uses *who.* The **a** versions below are the standard; the **b** sentences show the results of a consistent use of *whom:*

11.84a She is a woman whom we scarcely know.

b   She is a woman whom we scarcely know.

11.85a She is a woman who we know is punctual.

b   She is a woman whom we know is punctual.

11.86a I will ride with whom I choose.

b   I will ride with whom I choose.

11.87a They were talking about who would succeed us.

b   They were talking about whom would succeed us.

In some sentences, such as **11.84b** and **11.86b,** the selection of *whom* coincides with that of standard English; in others, such as **11.85b** and **11.87b,** *whom* reveals the speaker's confusion. For the person with only a smattering of knowledge about formal English grammar, the relative pronoun in **11.85** may seem to be the object of *know* rather than the subject of *is*. This sentence appears to be like **11.84,** in which the pronoun is, in fact, the object of *know*. Similarly, the pronoun seems to be the object of a preposition in both **11.86** and **11.87.** In the latter sentence, it is the entire noun clause that is the object of *about;* the pronoun *who* is the subject of *would succeed.* Without a clear understanding of the structure of a sentence, a person cannot select pronouns such as *who* and *whom* according to the principles of standard English.

Because of the tendency to make pronouns before the verb nominative and those after it objective, the predicate pronoun presents a special problem. Its position after the verb seems to indicate that an objective pronoun is required, yet generations of handbooks have given the nominative as the appropriate form because predicate pronouns (often called *predicate nominatives*) mean the same thing as the subject, which is nominative. They are also nominative in the classical languages. Yet, in spite of all the hard work of English teachers trying to teach people to say, "It is I," the usual form for unselfconscious speech remains "It's me." Presumably people would use "It is I" for formal writing, but this sentence occurs almost exclusively in informal conversation. With the other pronouns some people feel more comfortable with nominatives than they do with *I*. For example, if they were identifying people in a group photograph, they might say, "This is me," but "This is he. This is she. These are they." The last sounds more normal than "These are them," but either *he* and *she* or *him* and *her* would be possible for the singulars. For one structure, the subjunctive, we normally feel comfortable with the nominative case for predicate pronouns:

    11.88   If I were he, I would consult a lawyer.

To avoid a pronoun that stands out in formal usage, either because it is too informal (*This is him.*) or because it calls attention to itself for being too precise (*This is he.*), many writers avoid predicate pronouns altogether, replacing them with nouns or rewriting the sentence:

    11.89a   It is she who should go.
        b   She is the person who should go.

The **b** version avoids the problem.

STANDARDS OF USAGE

Learning that not all speakers of English use the same pronouns is interesting, but it is not very helpful when we have to use these forms in our writing or speaking. As there are no neutral forms, we have to make a choice. We cannot write sentences like these:

11.90   She was sitting between Gloria and $\left\{ \begin{array}{c} I \\ me \end{array} \right\}$.

11.91   Who(m) did you think it was?

Nor can we use *between you and I* in half our sentences and *between you and me* in the other half unless we do not mind being accused of inconsistency. After learning which forms other people use, we have to decide which ones are best for us.

It would be convenient if all choices in grammar could be given the simple labels "right" and "wrong." There are, in fact, many structures for which such labels are possible:

11.92   Emma Bovary is not a very intelligent woman.

11.93   *A woman not intelligent very is Emma Bovary.

We can easily place an asterisk before **11.93** and say that it is not a possible English sentence. Other choices, such as when to use *who* rather than *whom,* are not so straightforward.

All of us change our manner of speaking as we move from one audience to another. At one time of day we may be in a classroom discussing Chaucer's indebtedness to Boccaccio in *The Knight's Tale.* We then go into the hall and make arrangements with a friend for a ride home. After this we stand in line at the cafeteria and talk with a stranger about the weather. When we get home, we talk with members of the family, who may range in age from two to eighty. We sometimes have to ask each person to repeat a sentence: "What's that?" "What?" "Huh?" "Pardon me?" "Would you mind repeating that?" "Sir?" We unconsciously select the appropriate term according to the other person. We cannot select one term, such as "Sir?" or "Huh?" and say that it is always the "right" way to ask for repetition.

For most situations, we have developed a high level of proficiency in selecting the proper language; in fact, we are so proficient that we can forget about our sentences and concentrate on the conversation. The ability to select the proper forms did not always come to us painlessly. As children we learned that we could refer to our mothers as "Mommie" only among members of the family, not when we were playing with other children. Sometimes we were reprimanded for being too flippant and not showing respect for our elders when we used slang or other structures, such as "Yeah" and "Nope," or the positive and negative grunts "Uh huh, unh unh." Later, when our friends asked if we were going to play baseball that afternoon, we learned that "Yes, I think I shall" was not the appropriate response. If we did not want our friends to make fun of us, we had to use one of the responses for which our elders had reprimanded us.

By the time most people are in their late teens, they are skilled in selecting the appropriate language for the kinds of conversations that are most familiar to them. No textbook or teacher can help them improve these skills. It would be unfortunate if they misunderstood the textbook statements as moral dicta to be applied inflexibly at all times. Education is misguided if it makes people ashamed of their relatives and friends or lessens their ability to communicate with them.

The real value of the grammatical rules for pronouns and other structures is in their application to those situations which are relatively new to most people: professional speaking and formal writing. If employers demand a particular standard from their employees when they work with customers, anyone who wishes to hold one of these positions has to learn to speak in the prescribed manner. For everyone the language of interviewing, selling, banking, and the like is new at first; some have more adjustments to make than others. And written English is no one's native language. People who have read widely have usually acquired considerable proficiency in the written language, but everyone who learns to write well has to spend many hours acquiring the skill. The study of grammar will not help anyone with paragraphing, developing central theses, or organization. On the other hand, it can be indispensable in learning effective sentence structure, standard punctuation, and appropriate usage of pronouns and verbs. In many ways, acquiring the usage for formal situations is similar to learning a foreign language.

Once we recognize that there are differences in the ways people use language, how does that help us to choose between alternate forms such as *who* and *whom?* Let us look at a few examples. First, which of the following should we say?

11.94a   To whom did you send the chain letter?

   b   Who did you send the chain letter to?

Since we normally want people to react to our message, not our language, we would prefer that the person addressed merely respond with the appropriate answer. If this person also reacts with "Oh, how nice! *Whom!*" or "How slovenly! Ending a sentence with a preposition!" we have created a distraction. If we are trying to develop a sense of rapport with the other person, drawing attention to our language is unlikely to serve the purpose. Sentence **11.94a** is appropriate for formal situations, **11.94b** for those that are more casual. Both are good provided they are used at the proper time.

Here is a second situation in which we have to choose between *who* and *whom:*

11.95a   Who do you think paid for the dinner?

   b   Whom do you think paid for the dinner?

Since sentence **11.95b** will attract attention from everyone, it should be avoided. Unlike the two versions of **11.94,** which are right for some occasions, wrong for others, **11.95b** is always wrong. It shows that the speaker is trying to use standard English but has not succeeded.

For a third problem, let us look at a different pronoun:

11.96a   John and I will wash the car.

   b   Me and John will wash the car.

Although sentence **11.96b** is heard more often from children than from adults, some people use it all their lives. The structure would be inappropriate for formal usage, but people should not feel guilty if they use it among friends who also use this structure.

People who would like a simple "right" or "wrong" label for all matters of usage may feel like throwing up their hands in frustration when they are told that in a given sentence *who* is appropriate for some circumstances, *whom* for others. They may naively ask if we are not saying, "Anything goes." To the contrary, we are saying that language is more complex than they realize. In fact, we are saying that either *who* or *whom* can be wrong if used inappropriately, not that the two cases are interchangeable. In other aspects of language we recognize this kind of variability. For example, we call some people by nicknames (*Bobby*), others by full first names (*Robert*), others by titles and last names (*Mr. Anderson, Dr. Anderson*). Just as there is no single "right" form of address for all people in all circumstances, there is no single "right" use of *whom.* Human language is too complex to be described accurately with a few simple rules; people will be disappointed if they expect to find a set of rules that they can learn in thirty minutes and then apply inflexibly at all times. There are no shortcuts for the lazy.

When we discussed variant verb forms in Chapter 3, we noted that it is only a handful of verbs that show variation among speakers of English; for the vast majority of verbs, most people use the same past-tense and past-participial forms. A similar observation is true of pronouns and other structures. After reading several pages about problem cases, a person may overestimate their importance and number. For well over ninety percent of the sentences containing pronouns, there is widespread agreement among speakers and writers.

EXERCISES

A. Explain why the italicized pronouns and nouns can or cannot refer to the same person:

1. *Larry* laughed when *he* heard the announcement.
2. Because *she* was in such a rush, *Lottie* forgot her car keys.
3. *She* kicked the man who ridiculed *Dollie*.
4. Anyone who wants *them* may have *these cookies*.
5. *They* are especially courteous to anyone who leaves *those waiters* a big tip.

B. Replace the italicized noun phrases with pronouns that are appropriate for formal written English. If a sentence sounds artificial, revise it to avoid the problem.

1. In this world a person must do everything *a person* can to fight intolerance.
2. We invited everyone at the office to our Christmas party, and we hope *everyone at the office* can come.
3. Jeannie or I will let you see *Jeannie's* or my answers.
4. A member of the faculty wives' club announced that *a member of the faculty wives' club* would make the speech. [NB: The member who made the announcement is the one who will make the speech.]
5. Neither of the men will promise *neither of the men's* support.

C. In each of the following sentences, the italicized pronouns and nouns are supposed to refer to the same person. Explain what is wrong with the sentences marked with an asterisk; do not just correct them. Also explain why the choices of pronouns in the other sentences are correct.

1. *Nicole* is in love with *herself*.
2. **Those boys* invited *himself* to the party.
3. **Themselves* outsmarted *those men*.
4. *I* saw no one in the mirror except *myself*.
5. **I* detested the girl sitting behind *myself*.
6. *Charles* was told to protect *himself*.
7. Finding *herself* without any money didn't worry *Janice*.
8. **Ann told Frank* that it would be disastrous to marry *himself*.
9. **Paul* was believed to have cheated *him*.
10. **Congratulating yourself* will make people despise *yourself*.

195

D. Locate the reflexive pronouns in the following passage from James Boswell's *Life of Samuel Johnson* and explain how they follow the rules for reflexives given in this chapter:

> When we entered Mr. Dilly's drawing room, he [i.e., Johnson] found himself in the midst of a company he did not know. I kept myself snug and silent, watching how he would conduct himself. I observed him whispering to Mr. Dilly, "Who is that gentleman, Sir?" — "Mr. Arthur Lee." — JOHNSON, "Too, too, too" (under his breath), which was one of his habitual mutterings. ... "And who is the gentleman in lace?" — "Mr. Wilkes, Sir." This information confounded him still more; he had some difficulty to restrain himself, and taking up a book, sat down upon a window seat and read, or at least kept his eye upon it intently for some time, till he composed himself.

E. Select the pronouns that are appropriate for formal written English:

1. The stage manager and (she/her/herself) should have arranged those details.
2. Will they send it to you or (I/me)?
3. They opened the exhibit especially for (we/us) tennis players.
4. No one worked harder than (they/them/themselves).
5. The announcement pleased no one more than (he/him/himself).
6. Did they give you and (she/her) anything to eat?
7. He never had a kind word for my brother or (I/me/myself).
8. Was she the actress (who/whom) you read about?
9. Polly is the contestant (who/whom) everyone thinks will be chosen.
10. Who does he think wrote the note, Jenkins or (I/me/myself)?
11. The artist thanked Gerald and (he/him) for being so patient.
12. Would you apologize if you were (she/her)?
13. Can you sing as well as (he/him)?
14. The audience and (we/us) card players were all asked to leave immediately.
15. He shouted at (we/us) swimmers.
16. Everyone who tries to be nice to her — even her uncle and (I/me/myself) — is treated rudely.
17. Just between you and (I/me/myself), her poetry is miserable.
18. I have bought a box lunch for Cal and (I/me/myself).
19. She was sitting behind the losers, (he/him) and (I/me/myself).
20. (Who/whom) did you say they think should be fired?

F. Write *Acceptable* before those sentences that are appropriate for formal written English. Explain which changes are needed to make the others acceptable for this level of usage.

1. Nobody but him is interested in who is to be assigned the chairmanship.
2. The river had already overflown before we thought about who might still be in the house.
3. Do every one of you have a ride for tonight?
4. The new mayor is one of the most corrupt politicians that have ever been elected in this city.
5. He is the one whom everyone believed would finish last.
6. Every one of the women had requested some special pencils for their own use.
7. She wanted to have some free time so that she could lay in the sun for a few hours.
8. We have heard that neither the teachers nor the Dean is in favor of the new salary scale.
9. They tried to make it appear that we children were responsible for the confusion.
10. How could a simple boy like him refuse?
11. They could have beat the other team if they had been rested.
12. Which one of us did you want to see, Richard or me?
13. The English Building as well as all other buildings on that side of the campus was to be torn down.
14. Are you saying that she can type as fast as Lonnie or me?
15. The completion of the invitations and program guides have been more time consuming than anyone had realized.
16. She said that the ship sunk before everyone was rescued.
17. Has she showed you the new Administration Building?
18. Did you know that there is a man in a heavy overcoat and a woman in shorts waiting outside?
19. There, looking frightened, were the old woman and her six children.
20. Everyone in the class sat there looking as though they had never heard of Ruskin.

G. Assume that the following sentences are intended for conversation among professional people who speak standard English and also want to be cordial. Classify each sentence as appropriate, nonstandard, or pretentious.

1. He said that the house was for the use of Jack and I.

2. Anyone who agrees to work overtime should have their salary frozen.
3. I'm next on the list, aren't I?
4. I don't know about what you are talking.
5. The result of the investigations were that Compton was proved innocent.
6. He asked why I done it, but I didn't answer.
7. I, too. [Response to "I'm going to eat lunch in the cafeteria downstairs."]
8. The policeman told Harold and me to go home.
9. Whomever you nominate will be elected.
10. Who do you think I should send it to?

12

Sentence Structure and Complexity

In the last three chapters we noticed that some sentences are more difficult to understand than others. In Chapter 9, we said that a sentence may be clearer if a modifier is placed in one position rather than in another. Then in Chapters 10 and 11 we saw that compounding can obscure the structure so that people write phrases and clauses that are not parallel or hesitate over which pronoun to use. Even earlier, in Chapter 1 we said that the style of Hemingway strikes the reader as easier than that of Conrad because of the sentence structure. It seems appropriate, then, that this final chapter should review the ways in which sentence structure can increase or reduce complexity.

There are features other than sentence structure that make some sentences more difficult to understand than others, but they lie outside the scope of this book. For example, two accounts of the weather would differ considerably if one were written by a meteorologist and the other by a nonspecialist. Both might describe conditions during the same days, but the content and vocabulary would not be the same.

199

Also, some literary passages are harder for certain readers than for others. Shakespeare's sonnets, for example, are not especially difficult for the person accustomed to reading poetry; but to the student whose past exposure to poetry has been limited to works on the level of Joyce Kilmer's "Trees," these same sonnets may seem like something written in a foreign language. Many scholars have noticed that they had to learn to read certain writers almost the way they would another language: Henry James, William Faulkner, Gerard Manley Hopkins, William Butler Yeats, to name just a few. Yet those people who have spent many hours reading these writers and learned to appreciate them find them much less formidable because of the skills they have developed. They are like athletes who can do thirty push-ups without beginning to breathe heavily, whereas people in poor physical condition might find anything over five impossible.

As we speak of certain sentences being more complex than others, we do not mean that the good reader necessarily has trouble understanding them. The following sentences, for example, are presented in an order of increasing complexity:

12.1   "Tom touched his father on the shoulder." (John Steinbeck, *The Grapes of Wrath*]

12.2   "The town itself is dreary; not much is there except the cotton mill, the two-room houses where the workers live, and a few peach trees, a church with two colored windows, and a miserable main street only a hundred yards long." [Carson McCullers, *The Ballad of the Sad Cafe*]

12.3   "The fixer hurriedly travels on the train to Minsk and after months of desperate searching meets the old man, the moon on his rabbinic hat, coming home one evening from the synagogue." [Bernard Malamud, *The Fixer*]

12.4   "It was the summer after that first Christmas that Henry brought him home, the summer following the two days of that June vacation which he spent at Sutpen's Hundred before he rode on to the river to take the steamboat home, that summer after my aunt left and papa had to go away on business and I was sent out to Ellen (possibly my father chose Ellen as a refuge for me because at that time Thomas Sutpen was also absent) to stay so that she could take care of me, who had been born too late, born into some curious disjoint of my father's life and left on his (now twice) widowed hands, I competent enough to reach a kitchen shelf, count spoons and hem a sheet and measure milk into a churn yet good for nothing else, yet

> still too valuable to be left alone." [William Faulkner,
> *Absalom, Absalom!*]

Although the easiest sentence in this group is the shortest and the hardest is the longest, length alone is not the cause of the difficulty. To the person who has learned to read Faulkner, all four passages are comprehensible, and even the last requires no great strain. The differences among them are similar to those of the athletes who do five, ten, fifteen, or thirty push-ups. Although they can do any of these numbers, it still takes more effort to do thirty than it does to do five.

DISRUPTION OF THE SVO ORDER

The easiest sentences are those that are in the normal SVO order and that have no embedded or compound structures. There are several common processes that rearrange order, as the following sentences illustrate:

12.5   There were some ants in the breadbox.

12.6   Never have I heard anything so silly.

12.7   Whom did you tell?

Provided that the sentences are short, alterations of the SVO order such as these increase the complexity of the sentences only slightly; however, the fact that many people have trouble deciding whether to use a singular or plural verb in sentence 12.5 and *who* or *whom* in 12.7 shows that they are more difficult than the simple declaratives with SVO.

Rearrangements of word order for poetry also make sentences less straightforward. For example, the opening line of Robert Frost's "Stopping by Woods on a Snowy Evening" has an inversion:

12.8a   "Whose woods these are I think I know."

The normal order would have been:

12.8b   I think I know whose woods these are.

The line as Frost wrote it is obviously better poetry than the revision, but it is also less simple and may give trouble to the student who does not read well.

Let us compare a few lines from two poems to see how they differ in word order. Keats's sonnet "On First Looking into Chapman's Homer" begins like this:

> Much have I traveled in the realms of gold,
> And many goodly states and kingdoms seen;
> Round many western islands have I been
> Which bards in fealty to Apollo hold.

Since the poem describes an emotional response, it is rich in poetic diction and imagery. However, it is not just the choice of words and the allusions that set the tone; the word order is different from that found in prose. If we were asked to paraphrase the first four lines, keeping the same diction and imagery, we could write something like this:

> I have traveled much in the realms of gold,
> And seen many goodly states and kingdoms;
> I have been round many western islands
> Which bards hold in fealty to Apollo.

The lines no longer rime, and the meter has been changed for the worse; the content and imagery remain the same. What we have done is to revise the word order to that of Modern English prose so that a person who has not understood the lines will find them easier. In the first line we moved the adverb *much* after the verb *traveled* and positioned the subject before the verb, producing the following order:

Subject–Verb–Adverb of Frequency–Adverb of Place

In the second we placed the verb *seen* before its object. We made similar adjustments in the last two lines.

By contrast, Robert Frost's poem "The Death of the Hired Man" seems more commonplace:

> Mary sat musing on the lamp-flame at the table
> Waiting for Warren. When she heard his step,
> She ran on tip-toe down the darkened passage
> To meet him in the doorway with the news
> And put him on his guard. 'Silas is back.'

We notice an absence of poetic diction and mythological allusions, as is appropriate for lines describing simple physical actions. If we were asked to paraphrase these lines the way we did those by Keats, we would probably not be able to write anything simpler. The normal word order for Modern English prose is already present. This is one of the reasons that this poem by Frost seems easier than the sonnet we quoted by Keats.

EMBEDDED SENTENCES

Another source of sentence complexity is the presence of embedded sentences. Like the athletes who do a few push-ups, we hardly notice certain kinds of embedding:

> 12.9 When Roger took off his coat, we could see that he had been sweating.

Other kinds make sentences difficult to understand, and at times even incomprehensible. For example, we can start with a simple sentence like this:

> 12.10 The doctor frowned.

To explain which doctor we mean, we can introduce a relative clause based on the sentence *The patient hit the doctor:*

> 12.11a The doctor that the patient hit frowned.
>
> b The doctor the patient hit frowned.

The sentence is slightly easier with the relative pronoun included, as in **12.11a,** but both versions **a** and **b** are more difficult than **c:**

> 12.11c The doctor who was hit by the patient frowned.

Sentence **12.11b** is hard to understand but not impossible. If we add a relative clause to tell which patient did the hitting, based on *The nurse poked the patient,* the result is beyond the comprehension of most people:

> 12.12a The doctor the patient the nurse poked hit frowned.

If we revise the sentence to break up the series of three nouns followed by three verbs, the sentence is understandable:

> 12.12b The doctor who was hit by the patient that was poked by the nurse frowned.
>
> c The doctor frowned who was hit by the patient that the nurse poked.

It is not just embedding by itself that makes a sentence complicated; it is the kind of embedding.

Sentence **12.12c** illustrates a device that we often use to make sentences easier: extraposition. It would seem that this device would have the opposite effect because it moves some element, often the subject, out of its normal SVO position. However, for very long structures extraposition helps us to understand the sentence, as in the following example:

> **12.13a** "That when the Erewhonians profess themselves to be quite certain about any matter, and avow it as a base on which they are to build a system of practice, they seldom quite believe in it is a distinguishing peculiarity of the Erewhonians."

In this arrangement with the long subject noun clause in initial position, everyone finds the sentence virtually impossible. If we extrapose the subject noun clause, as Samuel Butler did in *Erewhon,* the sentence becomes clear:

> **12.13b** "It is a distinguishing peculiarity of the Erewhonians that when they profess themselves to be quite certain about any matter, and avow it as a base on which they are to build a system of practice, they seldom quite believe in it."

We also changed one instance of *the Erewhonians* to *they* in keeping with the rules for pronominalization, but this has nothing to do with sentence complexity. By extraposing the subject, we have marked out the structure, using the filler *it*. After indicating the structure, we then gave the long subject.

INTERRUPTIONS

Another means of changing the expected SVO order is to insert adverbials or parenthetical phrases within the sentence. For short sentences such interruptions are barely noticeable:

> **12.14a** *Next fall,* Albert will open a restaurant.
> **b** Albert will open a restaurant *next fall.*
> **c** Albert, *next fall,* will open a restaurant.

Even for short sentences adverbials that interrupt, as in the **c** version, make the sentence less natural than others such as **a** and **b.**

When the sentences are longer, such interruptions tend to make them more difficult. The following passage is from "The Tree of Knowledge" by Henry James, a writer who was fond of such interrupting devices:

> It was one of the secret opinions, such as we all have, of Peter Brench that his main success in life would have consisted in his never having

committed himself about the work, as it was called, of his friend Morgan Mallow. This was a subject on which it was, to the best of his belief, impossible with veracity to quote him, and it was nowhere on record that he had, in the connexion, on any occasion and in any embarrassment, either lied or spoken the truth.

Such as we all have comes between the noun *opinions* and its modifying prepositional phrase *of Peter Brench.* A similar clause, *as it was called,* separates *the work* from *of his friend Morgan Mallow.* Later, *to the best of his belief* separates the verb *was* from the predicate adjective *impossible.* And the long phrase *in the connexion, on any occasion and in any embarrassment* comes between the auxiliary *had* and its verb. The passage is less straightforward than it would have been if the order of the basic sentence elements had been left intact. We also notice the adverbial phrase *with veracity* preceding the infinitive *to quote,* rather than coming in the more basic order *to quote him with veracity.* James's positioning of adverbials and parenthetical phrases is one of the features that produce the effect readers describe as "complex" and "convoluted." To the person reading James for the first time, the word order may seem eccentric. After several readings of a short story such as "The Tree of Knowledge," however, the same reader usually comes to realize that although James's reasons for placing each phrase where he did are not always obvious, the story would suffer if they were left out.

Let us take another sentence from the same short story to see exactly what James did with it. We start with a simple sentence:

12.15a   Mrs. Mallow broke the news to their friend one day.

We next add an adverb clause to specify the day more exactly:

12.15b   Mrs. Mallow broke the news to their friend one day *when the boy was turning twenty.*

Now let us add a relative clause to modify *their friend:*

12.15c   Mrs. Mallow broke the news to their friend, *who shared their problems and pains,* one day when the boy was turning twenty.

The sentence is more complicated now, but we can still understand it with no difficulty. Let us next give the degree to which he shared the problems and pains: *to the last delicate morsel.*

12.15d   Mrs. Mallow broke the news to their friend, who shared their problems and pains *to the last delicate morsel,* one day when the boy was turning twenty.

With the long modifier for *friend,* the adverbial of time does not seem quite right at the end. We could move it to the beginning of the sentence:

12.15e   *One day when the boy was turning twenty,* Mrs. Mallow broke the news to their friend, who shared their problems and pains to the last delicate morsel.

However, this would not be in accordance with James's style. Instead, let us place this adverbial modifier between the subject and verb:

12.15f   Mrs. Mallow, *one day when the boy was turning twenty,* broke the news to their friend, who shared their problems and pains to the last delicate morsel.

And let us move *to the last delicate morsel* between the verb *shared* and its object:

12.15g   Mrs. Mallow, one day when the boy was turning twenty, broke the news to their friend, who shared, *to the last delicate morsel,* their problems and pains.

With the last two rearrangements (**12.15f** and **12.15g**), we have made the sentence more complicated than the **e** version, yet **g** sounds more like James than **e** does.

But we are not through. Let us explain what the news is: *that it seemed as if nothing would really do but that he should embrace the career.* Instead of *the news,* let us use this noun clause:

12.15h   Mrs. Mallow, one day when the boy was turning twenty, broke *that it seemed as if nothing would really do but that he should embrace the career* to their friend, who shared, to the last delicate morsel, their problems and pains.

Although James is often difficult, he is not unreadable. Let us, then, extrapose the object noun clause and fill its position with the expletive *it:*

12.15i   "Mrs. Mallow, one day when the boy was turning twenty, broke it to their friend, who shared, to the last delicate morsel, their problems and pains, that it seemed as if nothing would really do but that he should embrace the career."

We now have James's sentence.

HEMINGWAY AND CONRAD

In Chapter 1, after giving a passage by Hemingway and another by Conrad, we noticed that Hemingway's style seemed easier than Conrad's. We are now able to explain why. Both passages are repeated here. First, Hemingway:

> He felt of his knee. The pants were torn and the skin was barked. His hands were scraped and there were sand and cinders driven up under his nails. He went over to the edge of the track down the little slope to the water and washed his hands. He washed them carefully in the cold water, getting the dirt out from the nails. He squatted down and bathed his knee.

Then Conrad:

> It must be explained here that my cabin had the form of the capital letter L the door being within the angle and opening into the short part of the letter. A couch was to the left, the bed-place to the right; my writing-desk and the chronometers' table faced the door. But any one opening it, unless he stooped right inside, had no view of what I call the long (or vertical) part of the letter. It contained some lockers surmounted by a bookcase; and a few clothes, a thick jacket or two, caps, oilskin coat, and such like, hung on hooks. There was at the bottom of that part a door opening into my bath-room, which could be entered also directly from the saloon. But that way was never used.

The first difference that we notice is the length of the sentences. There are six sentences in each passage, but whereas the first contains only 71 words, the second has 131 — almost twice as many. We find a similar ratio if we compare the average number of words in the sentences of the two passages:

Hemingway *Sentence*	*Words*	*Conrad* *Sentence*	*Words*
1	5	1	31
2	9	2	20
3	15	3	25
4	20	4	26
5	15	5	23
6	7	6	6
Total	71	Total	131

207

The average number of words per sentence in the Hemingway passage is twelve, that in the Conrad twenty-two, again a ratio of almost 2:1. However, Hemingway does have some longer sentences, the fourth coming almost to Conrad's average; and Conrad's last sentence is shorter than most of those in the Hemingway passage. Yet even Hemingway's longer sentences seem much simpler than those by Conrad.

If we turn from length to the kinds of structures found in the sentences by the two writers, we see a major difference. Let us compare the embedded phrases and clauses:

Hemingway Sentence	Embedding
1	0
2	0
3	Past participial phrase
4	0
5	Present participial phrase
6	0

There are only two participial phrases in the Hemingway passage, no other phrases or clauses. In the Conrad passage we find more:

Conrad Sentence	Embedding
1	Noun clause, Absolute phrase (compound)
2	Absolute phrase
3	Present participial phrase, Adverb clause, Noun clause
4	Past participial phrase, Past participial phrase
5	Present participial phrase, Relative clause
6	0

Only the last sentence has no embedded structures; there are ten in the other five. In the Conrad passage most sentences have at least two embedded clauses or phrases, and in the fifth sentence the relative clause is embedded within the present participial phrase. In addition to the number of embedded structures, there is a rich variety. Whereas Conrad achieved his sentence length through embedding, Hemingway got his mainly through compounding (sentences two and three) or joining prepositional phrases (sentence four). It is the kinds of structures used by the authors that make their styles seem easy or complex, not the length of the sentences alone.

If we are talking about directions on a medicine bottle or similar uses of language, simpler sentences are preferable to the more complex, as long as both convey the same information. For other purposes, however, the simpler style may not always be the better. If most people tried to write in Hemingway's style, the result would sound choppy and childish. No one is interested in reading an account of modern problems in politics, the arts, or education if it sounds as though a child wrote it. Style can detract from the content to the point that people do not weigh the ideas. Hemingway was extremely successful in adapting his style to his content in a way that does not sound childish. If the content of a novel by Faulkner, James, or Conrad were attempted in a style such as Hemingway's, it is doubtful that anyone would care to read it. There are a great many intangible features that determine which style is best, not ease or complexity alone.

EXERCISES

A. Sentences 12.1–12.4 are listed in an order of increasing complexity. Explain what makes each one harder than the one before.

B. In this chapter we compared a passage from Hemingway with one from Conrad and explained why the latter seems more complex than the former. Make a similar comparison between the Conrad passage and the one from James quoted earlier in this chapter.

C. Read each of the following passages and classify it as easy, moderately difficult, or difficult. Then comment on the sentence structure to justify your classification.

  1. Tom Willard went briskly along the hallway and down a flight of stairs to the office. The woman in the darkness could hear him laughing and talking with a guest who was striving to wear away a dull evening by dozing in a chair by the office door. She returned to the door of her son's room. The weakness had passed from her body as by a miracle and she stepped boldly along. A thousand ideas raced through her head. When she heard the scraping of a chair and the sound of a pen scratching upon paper, she again turned and went back along the hallway to her own room. [Sherwood Anderson, *Winesburg, Ohio*]
  2. As, in gaining his place, some little perseverance, not to say persistence, of a mildly inoffensive sort, had been unavoidable, it was not with the best relish that the crowd regarded his apparent intrusion; and upon a more attentive survey, perceiving

no badge of authority about him, but rather something quite the contrary—he being of an aspect so singularly innocent; an aspect, too, which they took to be somehow inappropriate to the time and place, and inclining to the notion that his writing was of much the same sort: in short, taking him for some strange kind of simpleton, harmless enough, would he keep to himself, but not wholly unobnoxious as an intruder—they made no scruple to jostle him aside. [Herman Melville, *The Confidence Man*]

3. And the aged lord, without a word, shambled silently away, his old velvet shoes flapping and off at his heels, coughing as he went. As for Wang Lung, left alone with this woman, he did not know what to say or do. He was stupefied with the silence everywhere. He glanced into the next court and still there was no other person, and about the court he saw heaps of refuse and filth and scattered straw and branches of bamboo trees and dried pine needles and the dead stalks of flowers, as though not for a long time had anyone taken a broom to sweep it. [Pearl S. Buck, *The Good Earth*]

4. By ten-forty-five it was all over. The town was occupied, the defenders defeated, and the war finished. The invader had prepared for this campaign as carefully as he had for larger ones. On this Sunday morning the postman and the policeman had gone fishing in the boat of Mr. Corell, the popular storekeeper. He had lent them his trim sailboat for the day. The postman and the policeman were several miles at sea when they saw the small, dark transport, loaded with soldiers, go quietly past them. As officials of the town, this was definitely their business, and these two put about, but of course the battalion was in possession by the time they could make port. The policeman and the postman could not even get into their own offices in the Town Hall, and when they insisted on their rights they were taken prisoners of war and locked up in the town jail. [John Steinbeck, *The Moon Is Down*]

5. The affair being brought to this head, Mr. George, after a little consideration, proposed to go in first to his comrade (as he called him), taking Miss Flite with him. Mr. Bucket agreeing, they went away to the further end of the gallery, leaving us sitting and standing by a table covered with guns. Mr. Bucket took this opportunity of entering into a little light conversation, asking me if I were afraid of fire-arms, as most young ladies were; asking Richard if he were a good shot; asking Phil Squod which he considered the best of those rifles and

what it might be worth first-hand, telling him in return that it was a pity he ever gave way to his temper, for he was naturally so amiable that he might have been a young woman, and making himself generally agreeable. [Charles Dickens, *Bleak House*]

Index